Bloom's
GUIDES

John Knowles's
A Separate Peace

The Adventures of Huckleberry Finn

All the Pretty Horses

Animal Farm

The Autobiography of Malcolm X

The Awakening

Beloved

Beowulf

Brave New World

The Canterbury Tales

The Catcher in the Rye

The Chosen

The Crucible

Cry, the Beloved Country

Death of a Salesman

Fahrenheit 451

Frankenstein

The Glass Menagerie

The Grapes of Wrath

Great Expectations

The Great Gatsby

Hamlet

The Handmaid's Tale

The House on Mango Street

I Know Why the Caged Bird Sings

The Iliad

Invisible Man

Jane Eyre

Lord of the Flies

Macbeth

Maggie: A Girl of the Streets

The Member of the Wedding

The Metamorphosis

Native Son

1984

The Odyssey

Oedipus Rex

Of Mice and Men

One Hundred Years of Solitude

Pride and Prejudice

Ragtime

The Red Badge of Courage

Romeo and Juliet

The Scarlet Letter

A Separate Peace

Slaughterhouse-Five

Snow Falling on Cedars

The Stranger

A Streetcar Named Desire

The Sun Also Rises

A Tale of Two Cities

The Things They Carried

To Kill a Mockingbird

Uncle Tom's Cabin

The Waste Land

Wuthering Heights

Bloom's
GUIDES

John Knowles's
A Separate Peace

Edited & with an Introduction
by Harold Bloom

BLOOM'S
LITERARY CRITICISM
An imprint of Infobase Publishing

Bloom's Guides: A Separate Peace

Copyright © 2008 by Infobase Publishing

Introduction © 2008 by Harold Bloom

Bloom's Literary Criticism
An imprint of Infobase Publishing
132 West 31st Street
New York, NY 10001

Library of Congress Cataloging-in-Publication Data
John Knowles's A separate peace / edited & with an introduction by Harold Bloom.
    p. cm. — (Bloom's guides)
  Includes bibliographical references and index.
  ISBN 978-0-7910-9785-4 (acid-free paper)
  1. Knowles, John, 1926– Separate peace. 2. Preparatory school students in literature. I. Bloom, Harold. II. Title: Separate peace. III. Series.

PS3561.N68S436 2008
813'.54—dc22   2007040941

Contributing Editor: Amy Sickels
Cover design by Takeshi Takahashi
Printed in the United States of America
Bang EJB 10 9 8 7 6 5 4 3 2 1
This book is printed on acid-free paper.

Contents

120403

Introduction

HAROLD BLOOM

The paperback of John Knowles's *A Separate Peace* that I have just employed for rereading the novel, after nearly forty years, is in its ninety-eighth printing. Perpetually popular, *A Separate Peace* nevertheless is a Period Piece, though the period may go on a while longer, as it is most distinctly *the* Phillips Exeter Academy novel of our time, whatever our time turns out to be. Prep school fiction is its own genre, and Knowles certainly composed one of the few authentic classics in that necessarily limited mode.

Knowles has never matched *A Separate Peace*; his other novels and his short stories always seem in the wake of his first book. Finny, the tragic hero, is "too good to be true," as the narrator disarmingly remarks. Gene is more interesting and more culpable, skeptical, and finally destructive. If Finny is potentially Natural Man, or Original Virtue, Gene is a quester, never quite able to find himself, and deeply perplexed by his ambivalence toward Finny—an ambivalence that literally cripples his friend, crosses the border into repressed malice, and probably indicates some element, however displaced, of homoeroticism in Gene's stance toward poor Finny, though it would be an error to see that as centering the novel.

If Gene cannot bear Finny's innocence, neither can the mature reader, and so *A Separate Peace*'s peculiar merit is also its weakness: Finny cannot persuade us of his reality. One longs for him to manifest some flaw of spirit that might render him a touch more credible. Perhaps he needs a pinch of Scott Fitzgerald's Gatsby in him, but it is not there.

Unfortunately, Knowles could not resist the temptation of making Finny Christ-like, so that the tree from which he falls intimates the cross. The novel's greatest virtue, its lightness of style, cannot sustain the heavy symbolism.

That Finny's death should be a vicarious atonement for Gene, allowing the guilty friend to make the passage into maturity, fires too heavy a gun for this delicate narrative. Still, Knowles certainly found his audience for *A Separate Peace*, and perhaps the book will endure as long as prep schools do.

Biographical Sketch

John Knowles was born on September 16, 1926, in Fairmont, West Virginia, the third child of James Myron and Mary Beatrice Shea Knowles. His father was the vice president of the Consolidated Coal Company. When he was fifteen, Knowles left the hills of West Virginia to attend the Phillips Exeter Academy, a private boarding school in Exeter, New Hampshire, on which the Devon School in *A Separate Peace* is based. Knowles graduated from Phillips Exeter in 1945, and after graduating, he spent about eight months in the U.S. Army Air Force's Aviation Cadet Program. He then enrolled in Yale University, earning a bachelor's degree in English in 1949. While he was at Yale, he submitted short stories to the *Yale Record* and worked on the editorial staff for the undergraduate publication the *Yale Daily News*.

After graduating from Yale, Knowles landed a job at the *Hartford Courant*, working as a reporter and drama critic from 1950 to 1952, a position he left in 1952 to become a freelance writer. From 1952 to 1956, Knowles toured England, Italy, and France, earning his living as a journalist and freelance writer. Knowles befriended the playwright Thorton Wilder, a fellow Yale alumnus, who encouraged him in his vocation as a writer. During this time, Knowles wrote his first novel, the unpublished *Descent into Proselito*. He then moved to New York and began contributing to *Holiday* magazine. He published a number of short stories, including the short story "Phineas" in *Cosmopolitan*. This short story contains the basis for *A Separate Peace*.

In 1956, Knowles joined the *Holiday* staff as an associate editor. His first published novel, *A Separate Peace*, was released in 1959 in England and a year later Macmillan published the American edition to overwhelmingly favorable reviews. The novel was the winner of the Rosenthal Award of the National Institute of Arts and Letters and the William Faulkner Award for the most promising first novel of the year. It was also nominated for the National Book Award.

With the commercial success of *A Separate Peace*, Knowles was able to resign from his position at *Holiday* to devote himself to writing full time, and to embark on a two-year tour of Europe and the Middle East. His second novel, *Morning in Antibes*, the first of his Mediterranean novels, was published in 1962 while Knowles was still abroad. It was not as popular with the critics as *A Separate Peace*; in fact, none of Knowles's other novels was nearly as successful as his first published novel. In 1964, he published *Double Vision: American Thoughts Abroad*, a chronicle of his two-year travels.

Knowles returned to the United States in the early 1960s, though he continued to spend time abroad in between periods as writer-in-residence. He served as writer-in-residence at the University of North Carolina, Chapel Hill, from 1963 to 1964. His third novel, *Indian Summer*, was published in 1964 and became a Literary Guild Selection. Knowles dedicated the novel to his mentor, Thornton Wilder. From 1968 to 1969, Knowles served as writer-in-residence at Princeton University and published a short story collection, *Phineas: Six Stories*. Knowles's father died in 1970, the same year the writer took up permanent residence in Southampton, Long Island, in New York. He continued to write, publishing *The Paragon* (1971); *Spreading Fires* (1974); and *A Vein of Riches* (1978), a novel about the coal-mining business in West Virginia. The film version of *A Separate Peace* was released by Paramount Pictures in 1972. In 1978, Knowles donated his early longhand manuscripts to the Phillips Exeter Academy.

Knowles returned to the Devon School setting in *Peace Breaks Out* (1981), a companion novel to *A Separate Peace*. Since 1960, Knowles had published six more novels, none to the success or acclaim of *A Separate Peace*. In 1986, Knowles moved to Fort Lauderdale, Florida, and taught creative writing at Florida Atlantic University. John Knowles died on November 29, 2001, at a convalescent home in Fort Lauderdale after a short illness. He was seventy-five years old.

The Story Behind the Story

Eight years after J.D. Salinger's *A Catcher in the Rye* (1951) was published to widespread critical acclaim, another novel about a boys prep school appeared by a first-time novelist, and this one also garnered critical and popular success. Today, *A Separate Peace* continues to be one of the most widely read books in American schools, and has sold more than nine million copies to date. Though both *A Catcher in the Rye* and *A Separate Peace* focus on prep school boys who are coming of age, they are very different books—in style, structure, and subject matter.

In 1956, John Knowles was a staff writer for *Holiday* magazine, and he published a short article about his alma alter, the Phillips Exeter Academy in Exeter, New Hampshire. The trip he took back to the school inspired him to remember what it was like to be a student there during the time of World War II. Knowles pointed out that it was one of his happiest times in his life, and that his experiences at the all-boy prep school shaped and informed him. That same year, at age thirty, Knowles began writing *A Separate Peace*, the novel evolving from two of his short stories, "Phineas" and "A Turn in the Sun."

The setting for *A Separate Peace* is largely based on Exeter—including the Devon School, the rivers, the English-style buildings, and the playing fields. The time period, with World War II looming over the students, is also the same. Knowles drew on many of his own experiences for the plot, and modeled some of the characters on himself and his classmates. For example, the focus on scholarly work and athletics at Devon resembles the environment at Exeter. Also, Knowles and his friends had a club whose members jumped from the branch of a tree into the river as an initiation. Knowles participated in two consecutive summer sessions, in 1943 and 1944, a happy time for him. The war influenced everything, and in his novel, Knowles addresses some of the issues that came up: "And what was war, and what was aggression, and what were loyalty and rivalry, what were goodness and hate and fear and idealism, all of them swirling around us during that peculiar summer?" (*Esquire*, March 1985.)

Though Knowles drew on personal experiences and memories, none of the major incidents in *A Separate Peace* were based on reality, including Gene's jealousy or Finny's fall. Knowles's summer at Devon was a time of friendship and loyalty, and did not contain the elements of violence, anger, and envy that drive the plot of his novel. Knowles modeled Phineas on his friend, David Hackett, an exceptional athlete. Though they were in school together for only one summer, Hackett left a lasting impression on Knowles, and later served under Robert F. Kennedy in the Justice Department in Washington D.C. But, Hackett did not fall from a tree. Instead, Knowles turned a minor accident that had happened to him into a fateful one for Finny, explaining, "This reversal made it possible to show the darker streaks of human nature. If I were going to make my point, then the Phineas character would have to be the victim" (*Esquire*, March 1985.) Brinker Hadley was based on the famous author Gore Vidal, who was a senior at Exeter when Knowles was a sophomore. Like most authors, Knowles drew on parts of himself in each of the four main characters. He explained, "The book is autobiographical. By no means did all the incidents happen as portrayed, but the emotional truth of it comes to life" (*Esquire*, March 1985.)

A Separate Peace was first published in England, where it received positive reviews. A year later, in 1960, Macmillan published the first American edition. Although *A Separate Peace* did not become an instant best-seller—selling only 7,000 copies in its first American printing—it gradually became a commercial success. At the time of its publication, critics praised the novel and Knowles was hailed as a successor to J.D. Salinger. The novel won the first William Faulkner Award for notable first novel and received the 1960 Rosenthal Award of the National Institute of Arts and Letters. The book would eventually become a minor American classic.

After *A Separate Peace*, Knowles published more novels, including *Peace Breaks Out*, a companion novel to *A Separate Peace*. However, none of his later works ever received even a fraction of the acclaim as *A Separate Peace*, which would always be his crowning achievement. Knowles did not seem to be bothered by the fact that his other novels remained unknown. He felt grateful for the success of *A Separate Peace* because it freed him from having to work a second job; he could devote himself full time to writing.

A Separate Peace continues to be one of most widely taught books in American high schools. Despite the dark tone and pessimistic view of the human condition, the novel offers ultimately a positive and nostalgic perspective of adolescence.

List of Characters

Gene Forrester is the narrator/protagonist. When the novel begins, Gene is in his early thirties, visiting the Devon school for the first time in fifteen years. For the majority of the novel, Gene is a sixteen- and seventeen-year-old student during World War II. Gene is one of the top students in the class and also a talented athlete. He is best friends with Finny. However, his love and admiration for Finny are marred by his fierce jealousy and competitive nature. Gene is quiet, intelligent, and brooding. He is sometimes a reticent and unreliable narrator, and his internal emotional battles are a major source of tension in the novel. By the end, Gene lets go of his jealousy and reaches a more profound understanding of himself and humankind.

Phineas (Finny) is Gene's classmate and best friend. He is by far Devon's best athlete. He is also charismatic, well liked, and persuasive. Though he often breaks the rules at Devon, he never gets into trouble, easily talking his way out of it. Finny is not nearly as strong a student as Gene, however, he possesses none of Gene's jealousy or competitive nature. Finny is honest and loyal, and almost too good to be true. He represents innocence and goodness, and never perceives anyone to be his enemy. However, after breaking his leg, Finny must face his own personal struggle, and eventually, admits to the fall of man.

Brinker Hadley, first introduced in the Winter Session, is in some ways a foil to Finny's character. He is a charismatic student leader, but his devotion is to order and rules, while Finny's is to spontaneity and fun. Brinker believes in justice and discovering the truth. His name is symbolic, as he tends to push people "to the brink"; this is demonstrated many times in the book, most obviously during the trial. Over the course of the year, Brinker becomes disillusioned and less active in school organizations.

Elwin "Leper" Lepellier would rather spend his time cross-country skiing and searching for beaver dams than participating in games with the other boys. He is a loner, who is gentle, dreamy, and peaceful. He was present when Finny "fell" from the tree. Leper is the first of the Devon boys to enlist in the army, where he suffers a breakdown.

Cliff Quackenbush is the manager of the crew team. He is gruff, bitter, and not well liked by the other students. He takes advantage of Gene's position as assistant crew manager, using it as an opportunity to treat someone as an inferior, but Gene fights back.

Chet Douglass is Gene's main rival for the position of class valedictorian. Chet possesses a sincere love of learning. He remains on the periphery of the novel.

Dr. Stanpole is Devon's resident doctor. He takes care of Finny after both of his accidents.

Mr. Hadley, appearing in the last chapter, is Brinker's father. He is an example of the war enthusiast of the older generation, and is disappointed that his son and Gene want to stay away from combat.

Mr. Ludsbury is the authoritative Master of Winter Session. He encourages Gene and Finny to abandon their Olympic training to focus instead on preparing themselves for the war.

Summary and Analysis

1

A Separate Peace is a coming-of-age novel set at a private boys' boarding school in New Hampshire during World War II. The novel uses Christian and Greek symbols, and themes of war and peace, to depict the fallen condition of man. The narrator and protagonist, Gene Forrester, must face both the reality of the war that is raging across Europe and the darkness within his own heart. The novel chronicles Gene's betrayal, his fall from grace, and redemption. *A Separate Peace* is a war novel that does not take place on the battlefield, but depicts the impact of war on the minds and sensibilities of people who are not yet directly involved. The Devon School, "scholarly and very athletic," represents a separate peace, a shelter from the war, yet over the course of the novel, Knowles reveals how even the innocence and beauty of a prep school cannot escape the horror.

A Separate Peace, of course, is also about friendship and betrayal. Gene and Finny appear to be close friends, but, as Gene recounts their story, he begins to reveal his complicated feelings of love/hate toward Finny. Beneath their seemingly close friendship in these tranquil surroundings lurks Gene's jealousy, and eventually, his destruction.

The novel occurs in thirteen chapters, over a period of a school year. In the first three chapters, Gene's feelings of envy and resentment toward Finny build until the fourth chapter, the climax of the first part, in which Finny falls from the tree, ending the peaceful, Edenic summer. Chapters 5–10 depict the starkness of Devon in the winter session, and reveal Finny's growing dependency on Gene. The tension increases as the illusions of peace and innocence are chipped away, until the climactic makeshift trial in Chapter 11, when Gene stands accused. Finny's second fall at the end of the novel propels Gene to face the truth and brings him to a greater understanding; the final two chapters focus on his maturity and the end of his boyhood.

2

The novel begins in 1957, fifteen years after the main events. Gene Forrester, the narrator/protagonist, is visiting the Devon School for the first time since he graduated. It is presumed that now, at thirty-two, Gene can look back at his life at Devon with more clarity, understanding how key events unfolded and shaped him into the man he is now. The voice and structure is immediately established; the reader understands that Gene has put things into perspective since graduating from Devon.

Knowles's choice of the first person point of view has been widely analyzed by critics. The first person point of view allows the audience to be close to Gene; however, at the same time, Gene's voice is distant and controlled, creating a sense of detachment. The readers do not learn much about the adult Gene, except that he now has "more money and success." It is a mature voice, much different than say, the first person narrator in J.D. Salinger's *The Catcher in the Rye*. While Holden Caulfield's voice is an emotional teenager's voice that gives the reader a sense of immediacy, the first person point of view employed in *A Separate Peace* more closely resembles the voice of Nick Carraway in Scott Fitzgerald's *The Great Gatsby*. The critic Ronald Weber describes Gene's voice as "dispassionate, reflective, and controlled; it is, in his own words, a voice from which fury is gone, dried up at its source long before the telling begins" (68). Looking back, presumably from a perspective of greater maturity and wisdom, Gene can clearly see how fear had barred him from facing himself: "Looking back now across fifteen years, I could see with great clarity the fear I had lived in, which must mean that in the interval I had succeeded in a very important understanding: I must have made my escape from it."

Gene walks around Devon, still "the most beautiful school in New England," but perceives it in a different way than he had expected, as if a coat of varnish had been applied to the buildings: "I didn't entirely like this glossy new surface, because it made the school look like a museum, and that's exactly what it was to me, and what I did not want it to be." Gene had hoped to feel that time has passed, maybe even been erased, but instead the past is preserved, like a museum.

His quiet, controlled voice also establishes a mood of dread—Gene doesn't give anything away, but makes vague references, hinting to the darkness to come: "Contributing to the irony established by the disjuncture of cause and effect, or setting and event, is Knowles's quiet understated style. That violence should leap so suddenly out of Knowles's offhand, conversational cadences sharpens the horror of the violence" (Wolfe 191).

Gene visits the two "fearful sites" on campus, foreshadowing their importance. When he goes to the First Academy building, he notices how hard the marble floor is: "It was surprising that I had overlooked that, that crucial fact." This comment, which does not yet hold relevance to the reader, adds suspense. The tree itself, past the playing fields, stands next to the Devon River. Gene is surprised, and relieved, that this tree, which holds such powerful memories for him, seems diminished: "It had loomed in my memory as a huge lone spike dominating the riverbank, forbidding as an artillery piece, high as the beanstalk. Yet here was a scattered grove of trees, none of them of any particular grandeur." The tree has lost its significance and power. It is no longer a gigantic looming tower, but is now one of many trees.

Gene looks at the tree and thinks, "Nothing endures, not a tree, not love, not even a death by violence," a resonating theme that is realized in Gene's dark journey from boyhood to adulthood. The reference to "a death by violence" works as a foreshadowing device, contributing to the atmosphere of dread. Gene leaves the "fearful" tree, and goes back the way he came: "Changed, I headed back through the mud. I was drenched; anybody could see it was time to come in out of the rain." Gene can be satisfied that he has moved on, that though the memory lives with him, it does not control him. He has let go of fear, and faced his true self. He is "changed." No longer drenched in the past, he comes in out of the rain.

After these first few pages in Chapter 1, the narrative switches to the year 1942, when Gene was a student at Devon and the world is caught up in the events of World War II. This flashback beings midway through Chapter 1, and lasts through the entire novel. It starts with a contrasting description of the tree: "The tree was tremendous, an irate, steely black steeple beside the river." Though still in the first person point of view, the description of the tree now establishes a shift in the time and the mood. We are now back in the early 1940s. The tree, from a sixteen year old's perspective, is frightening.

With the switch in time, the narration now seems to be told from the younger Gene, yet the older narrator continues to insert commentary. It is a complex narrative voice, capturing both the adolescent and adult perceptions. Furthermore, Gene's tendency to recount external events but to be less forthcoming about his desires and emotions adds another level of tension to the novel. Gene cannot be counted on as a reliable narrator, as the critic James L. McDonald points out: "Thus the reader's judgments are not always the same as the narrator's; and so the reader is led to question the narrator's motives and interpretations. Should Forrester be taken at his own evaluation?" (336) Peter Wolfe adds, "His first-person narration is laced with self-abuse, special pleading, flawed logic, and evasiveness" (191). The reader cannot take what Gene says at face-value, but must read between the lines.

Gene, his roommate Phineas (who the boys call Finny), and three other boys—Elwin "Leper" Lepellier, Chet Douglass, and Bobby Zane—are gathered at the "fearful" tree. The boys are participating in the Devon summer session, "in shaky transit," between being Lower Middlers to Upper Middlers (seniors), also known as "draft-bait." Though the boys realize that next year they too will be a part of the war, for now they are encouraged to enjoy their boyhood. Although the war informs their lives, as seen in their many references to it, within this "gypsy summer" they are still boys, "calmly, numbly reading Virgil and playing tag in the river further downstream."

It is Finny's idea that the boys jump from the tree into the river, a feat that no student their age has tried before. The older boys must jump as a part of their war training regiment. For Finny, it is a simply an athletic challenge and pure thrill. Outgoing and persuasive, with a voice that is "the equivalent in sound of a hypnotist's eyes," Finny climbs the tree, walks out onto the branch, and jumps into the Devon River. "Well," he cried out, "here's my contribution to the war effort!" Finny "plays" at war, which for him, will only ever be a game. Finny represents boyhood and innocence. His name, Phineas, resembles the name Phoebus Apollo, the god of light and youth.

After Finny jumps, he asks who is next. The other boys worry about breaking the rules and do not rise to the challenge. Gene is terrified, but he climbs the tree anyway, "with a sensation of alarm all the way to my tingling fingers," and Finny orders Gene to jump, "shaming" him into it. When Gene hears Finny yell "Jump," he feels resentful: "Why did I let Finny talk me into stupid things like this? Was he getting some kind of hold over me?" Gene never voices his doubts or fears to Finny, and this first jump reveals that Gene is a loyal yet secretly critical follower of Finny. He feels captive to Finny's persuasive power, his disregard for rules, his joy for life, and his fearlessness. Gene often makes references to Finny's admirable traits, hinting that he wants to emulate Finny, to be able to do whatever Finny can do. Gene follows Finny's jump with "the sensation that I was throwing my life away." This plunge from the tree into the Devon River in Chapter 1 is contrasted later in Chapter 6, when Gene falls into the Naguamsett River, the Devon's opposite. Both scenes symbolize a different kind of baptism. Now, with his jump into the Devon, the baptism is a celebration of freedom and innocence, and he and Finny appear to be on equal footing. The experience bonds them, an act of trust and intimacy: "We were the best of friends at that moment."

Finny is by far Devon's best athlete, seeming to possess a natural physical harmony with his body and the world around him. When he walks, he "flowed on" like water, "rolling forward in his white sneakers with such unthinking unity of movement." In Gene's view, everything about Finny flows, not just physically, but emotionally as well. In fact, Finny seems to possess all good traits. He is handsome, charismatic, well liked, modest, and charming. Though he often breaks the rules at Devon, he never gets into trouble because he can easily talk his way out of it.

On the walk to dinner, Gene breaks into his "West Point stride," worried that they'll be late, but Phineas trips him and they engage in a brief scuffle. As they continue on with their walk, Gene feels himself "hurrying and conforming." He resents this aspect of himself, and wants to be more like Finny. So, "I threw my hip against his, catching him by surprise, and he was instantly down, definitely pleased. This was why he liked me so much."

Knowles depicts Finny and Gene as opposites, highlighting their contrasts, as he also does with the other pairs in the novel—the seasons, the rivers, the school versus the outside. While Finny is the rule-breaker, the outgoing one, the stellar athlete, Gene is more of a follower, the studious one. Because their personalities contrast, it is possible that they could find a harmonious balance, a yin and yang. Yet, Finny's personality is so much stronger than Gene's that the relationship falls out of balance. Instead of feeling secure in his own personality, Gene wants to be like Finny, viewing him as superior. Because of this, he begins to resent Finny. The reader soon understands that the dynamics between Gene and Finny are complex, and that it is not the simple friendship Gene attempts to portray in Chapter 1; there are subtle hints of something darker underneath. Gene alludes often to Finny's grace, charm, and handsome looks, presenting his qualities as if he is simply annoyed by Finny's superiorities; yet, in Chapters 2–4, the reader realizes that he harbors a much deeper envy.

3

Chapters 1 through 4 take place during the summer session, in which the atmosphere, instead of the usual Devon austerity, is relaxed. The "gypsy" summer represents innocence and freedom, bordering on chaos. The school masters loosen their reign, and look the other way when rules are broken. "I think we reminded them of what peace was like, we boys of sixteen," Gene muses. While the older boys train for the war, Gene, Finny, and their classmates linger in boyhood, enjoying the illusory peace while they still can. "We reminded them of what peace was like, of lives which were not bound up with destruction," states Gene, although the reader later realizes the irony in this statement.

One of the narrative tensions expressed throughout the novel is the thin line between reality and illusion, and war and peace. For now, instead of worrying about the war, the boys swim in the river, play games, skip meals, and bask in the glorious summer. "We were careless and wild, and I suppose we could be thought of as a sign of the life the war was being fought to preserve." Critic James Mellard attests: "As long as the summer lasts, the sense of peace and fulfillment and happiness conquers the encroachments of the war, with its defeats, frustrations and pain" (128). Like all Americans, the boys are exposed to the "thousand newspaper photographs and newsreels." But as Gene claims, "our place here was too fair for us to accept something like that." However, as the narrative continues, it is revealed that although the summer represents a time of peace, Gene is not at peace with himself.

The relaxed rules at Devon, combined with Finny's ability to talk his way out of trouble, provide the boys with a sense of freedom. In Chapter 2, when Gene and Finny are approached by Mr. Prud'homme for skipping dinner, it is Finny's charming and "scatterbrained" powers of persuasion that cause the master to lose "his grip on sternness." The teachers are never able to stay angry with Finny, who is not a bad kid, combining "a calm ignorance of the rules with a winning urge to be good." Finny disregards rules, but never lies: "everything he said was true and sincere; Finny always said what he happened to be thinking, and if this stunned people then he was surprised." Finny loves the school deeply, and is loyal to Devon and his classmates, yet he is no scholar, and feels "most comfortable in the truant's corner." Gene admires Finny's charm and honesty, yet is jealous of the ease with which Finny wins over the teachers and students.

When Finny wears a "very pink" shirt, Gene objects, "It makes you look like a *fairy*!" But Finny only responds, "Does it?" in the "preoccupied tone [he used] when he was thinking of something more interesting than what you had said." Gene is overly concerned with how others perceive him, whereas

Finny does not seem to care about conforming to social norms. Unlike Gene, Finny doesn't care what others think. He muses, "I wonder what would happen if I looked like a fairy to everyone." Gene takes note of how Finny wears the pink shirt around school, but no one teases him. "No one else in the school could have done so without some risk of having it torn from his back."

Gene decides, "It was hypnotism. I was beginning to see that Phineas could get away with anything. I couldn't help envying him that a little, which was perfectly normal. There was no harm in envying even your best friend a little." Gene tries to sound nonchalant, justifying his jealousy, but he also reveals to the reader that something is flawed in his friendship with Finny.

Chapter 2 continues with Finny charming his way out of trouble. At the headmaster's house, he is discovered to be using the school tie for a belt, and Gene thinks, "This time he wasn't going to get away with it. I could feel myself becoming unexpectedly excited at that." Yet Finny rises to the moment by giving a long-winded, confusing answer about the tie and its connection to the war. Mr. Patch-Withers seems baffled, and yet to his disappointment, Gene realizes that "Phineas was going to get away with even this."

Throughout Chapters 2–4 Gene's jealousy becomes more apparent to the reader. At times, he seems to be trying to convince himself (and the readers) that he is right in his feelings, and that he did actually not want Finny to suffer. "He had gotten away with everything. I felt a sudden stab of disappointment. That was because I just wanted to see some more excitement; that must have been it." This last line, "that must have been it," is a telling example of Gene's attempt to convince himself. The reader must read between the lines to understand that maybe Gene did want his friend to get into trouble, to suffer. As an unreliable narrator, he is sometimes hard to pin down. How much information is he giving to the reader, and what is he withholding?

Toward the end of Chapter 2, Finny creates the Super Suicide Society of the Summer Session, in which the initiation is to jump out of the tree. This time when he and Gene climb the tree, Gene loses his balance, and Finny's hand shoots out and grabs him: "Finny had practically saved my life." This scene concludes the chapter, paralleling the end of Chapter 4, when Finny falls, and also establishing a sharp contrast in Gene and Finny's loyalty toward each other.

Chapter 3 opens with the line, "Yes, he had practically saved my life. He had also practically lost it for me. I wouldn't have been on that damn limb except for him." Instead of being grateful, Gene turns the moment into an opportunity to blame Finny, which exemplifies Gene's growing feelings of resentment. Using his calm, rationalizing voice, he attempts to persuade us that Finny is to blame, but instead, reveals his own selfishness.

On the surface, Gene acts the same—he gives no hint to Finny or the others that he feels anything but benevolence toward Finny. He continues to attend the Super Suicide Society meetings, which Finny holds every night. The club now includes six other boys. Finny makes up arbitrary rules about the club; one of rules is that Gene and Finny kick off every meeting by jumping from the tree.

"I hated it," Gene states, an admission he never shares with Finny. "But I always jumped. Otherwise I would have lost face with Phineas, and that would have been unthinkable." Gene's fear of losing Finny's respect, and his need to keep up appearances, overpower his true feelings. "I went along; I never missed a meeting. At that time it would have never occurred to me to say, "I don't feel like it tonight," which was the plain truth every night."

Finny is only shown through Gene's perspective. Most readers, like the other boys, are won over by Finny's clever personality, his obvious devotion to Gene, and his enthusiasm for life. Critics of Knowles have pointed out that Finny seems unbelievable because he is flawless—charismatic, loyal, athletic, and modest. Yet he is also extremely self-involved, which will be his fatal flaw. Finny fails to perceive how others around him feel, and how they might think differently from him. For instance, he never stops to consider that Gene might not want to leap from the tree. But of course, Gene never says anything either, so the truth is never brought out into the open.

Finny, who loves sports above all else, is disgusted by the summer's meager athletic program, especially with badminton. One day, Finny spontaneously creates "blitzball," and Gene sees that "he had unconsciously invented a game which brought his own athletic gifts to their highest pitch." The game involves a medicine ball; there are no teams, or winners or losers. Finny, unlike Gene, does not believe in competition, and in his view, nobody ever loses at sports: "Nothing bad ever happened in sports; they were the absolute good." Blitzball, named after the Blitz, which was the sustained bombing of the United Kingdom by Nazi Germany, is an example of how the war influences the boys' world of games and play.

Finny's lack of competitive spirit is also demonstrated in Chapter 3 when he breaks the school swim record on his first attempt. Gene, the only witness to this amazing feat, feels troubled by Finny's reaction. Instead of gloating, or showing any sense of pride, Finny orders Gene not to tell anyone about his accomplishment. Whereas Gene needs conventional approval and support, Finny cares only about the sport itself, not the accomplishment or competition. For Gene, this is another example of how Finny is superior to him: "You're too good to be true." This episode grows in Gene's mind, and darkens his feelings toward Finny: "Perhaps for that reason his accomplishment took root in my mind and grew rapidly in the darkness where I was forced to hide it."

After breaking the record, Finny decides they should go to the beach "hours away by bicycle, forbidden, completely out of all bounds." Gene does not want to go; he knows they are risking expulsion, and not only that, he has a trigonometry test the next morning. He is also opposed to the idea because it "blasted the reasonable amount of order I wanted to maintain in my life." Gene needs to control life, whereas Finny heads toward chaos.

Instead of refusing Finny, Gene goes along on the trip; Finny does not detect that Gene does not want to be there. Along the way, Finny is in high spirits, playful and performing tricks on his bike. Once they reach the ocean, he spends the time laughing, swimming, and entertaining Gene: "And he did everything he could think of for me."

Some critics have pointed out that Finny and Gene's relationship may be homoerotic, or contain elements of homosexuality. The only time homosexuality is directly mentioned is in Chapter 2, when Gene is afraid that Finny will be called a fairy if he wears the pink shirt. Gene, then, is afraid of being seen as gay but Finny does not seem to worry. Gene often mentions Finny's handsome looks, especially in this scene at the beach:

> I noticed that people were looking fixedly at him, so I took a look myself to see why. His skin radiated a reddish copper glow of tan, his brown hair had been a little bleached by the sun, and I noticed that the tan made his eyes shine with a cool blue-green fire.

But, Finny quickly takes the moment to tell Gene "Everybody's staring at you. . . . It's because of that movie-star tan you picked up this afternoon . . . showing off again." It seems that even if the relationship is not sexual, it is strongly physical, with elements of attraction.

The boys spend the night, sleeping on the beach. Before they fall asleep, Finny tells Gene that he is his best friend. The reader empathizes with Finny; we believe that he cares for Gene. Instead of returning the sentiment, however, Gene stays silent, refusing to expose himself:

> It was a courageous thing to say. Exposing a sincere emotion nakedly like that at the Devon School was the next thing to suicide. I should have told him that he was my best friend also and rounded off what he had said. I started to; I nearly did. But something held me back. Perhaps I was stopped by that level of feeling, deeper than thought, which contains the truth.

Gene fears what others would think if they found out about this kind of affection; but there is something else stopping him: as the readers have learned, Gene cannot reciprocate Finny's feelings because his own are tainted with envy. This scene, which ends the chapter, exemplifies how Gene is divided between admiration and resentment toward Finny. He holds back because though he truly cares about Finny, he also harbors a growing dislike toward him.

4

Chapter 4 is the climactic chapter in the book, in which Finny falls from the tree. The events leading up to this scene show Gene at his most vicious. His resentment toward Finny turns into paranoia, and he tries overcomes his shame for his envy and insecurity by convincing himself that Finny feels the same toward him.

Chapter 4 begins on the beach. Gene wakes up and notices Finny "still asleep, although in this drained light he looked more dead than asleep," a line that hints at darker things to come. Gene and Finny make it back to Devon in time for Gene's ten o'clock trigonometry test, but he fails it, the first test he's ever flunked. His resentment and jealousy can no longer be contained.

Finny jokes that Gene wants to be the class valedictorian, though Gene will not admit it, he realizes this is true—he wants to be better than Finny at something. When he asks Finny what he would do if he were head of the class, Finny jokes, "I'd kill myself out of jealous envy," but Gene believes him: "The joking manner was a screen; I believed him." However, the reader understands that Finny is joking, that Gene's feelings are misguided.

It is in this chapter that Gene's darkness fully rises to the surface, contrasting to the idyllic summer mood. Gene must force himself to maintain his hate by inventing Finny's motivations:

> I found a single sustaining thought. The thought was, You and Phineas are even already. You are even in enmity. You are both coldly driving ahead for yourselves alone. You did hate him for breaking that school swimming record,

but so what? He hated you for getting an A in every course but one last term. You should have had an A in that one except for him. Except for him.

The reader knows that Finny does not view Gene in these terms, but, in order to accept his own feelings, Gene must convince himself that Finny also harbors jealousy. He decides that Finny planned the trip to the beach on purpose, in order to ruin his academic career: "Then a second realization broke as clearly and bleakly as dawn at the beach. Finny had deliberately set out to wreck my studies."

This is a turning point for Gene; by convincing himself that they are competitors and enemies, Gene feels better about coming to terms with his true feelings. "Yes, I sensed it like the sweat of relief when nausea passes away; I felt better. We were even after all, even in enmity. The deadly rivalry was on both sides after all." The stinging actuality, however, is that Finny does not view Gene as his enemy; the discrepancy then, between reality and Gene's inner thoughts, creates a tension of dread and doom.

After this invented realization, Gene becomes more dedicated to his studies, so that he can become head of the class, hoping to surpass Chet Douglass, who, unlike Gene, loves learning. Gene studies because he wants to win; he needs awards and rewards, and he wants to beat Finny at something. "I was more and more certainly becoming the best student in the school; Phineas was without question the best athlete, so in that way we were even. But while he was a very poor student I was a pretty good athlete, and when everything was thrown into the scales they would in the end tilt definitely toward me."

During this period, Finny and Gene get along well, so that at times, Gene occasionally doubts himself. "Sometimes I found it hard to remember his treachery, sometimes I discovered myself thoughtlessly slipping back into affection for him again." The Suicide Society continues to meet each evening, and Gene attends because "I didn't want Finny to understand me as I understood him." Gene hides his feelings from Finny and the others, so that nobody suspects that anything is amiss in their friendship.

Then one night when Gene is studying for a French test, Finny comes into the room and announces that Gene needs to come down to the tree because Leper is planning to jump. Gene doesn't believe it, and decides that Finny is saying this only to interrupt his studies. When Gene slams the book closed in anger, Finny asks what's wrong. At first, Gene doesn't believe him: "What a performance! His face was completely questioning and candid." Gene begins to storm out, but Finny, concerned, tells him not to come; he admires Gene's intelligence, and didn't realize until now that Gene needed to study. He tells Gene he's right to stay, and urges him to stick with his studies: "Don't go, it's fine. What the hell, it's only a game."

But Gene, unnerved by Finny's response, tells him he has studied enough, and goes with him to the tree. Gene now understands what the reader already knew: "He had never been jealous of me for a second. Now I knew that there never was and never could have been any rivalry between us. I was not of the same quality as he. I couldn't stand this." Before this moment, Gene was jealous of Finny's popularity, his ability to get away with things, and his athleticism and charm. But now he believes that Finny is morally superior, and this pushes Gene over the edge. He envies Finny's goodness, and it is too much for him to bear:

> It is Phineas's innocence that Gene cannot endure. As long as he can believe Phineas shares his enmity, he can find relief; but with this assurance gone, he stands condemned before himself and must strike out against his tormenter. Fear, again, is the key word. Fear in his instance is the emotional response to the discovery of hate, the vast depths of enmity that exist within the human heart. (Weber 70).

Until this point, all of the darkness has been stored inside of Gene. But now he realizes the difference between him and Finny: "The fundamental contrast is simply that Gene is all too human heir to all the weakness of flesh and spirit, while Finny, at least as Gene sees him most of the time, is little less than a divinity. Thus where Gene is at times morally and ethically shallow, Finny is the epitome of honesty and openness and facility" (Mellard 130).

Moments later, Gene and Finny climb the tree to perform a double jump, which Finny wants to do as a symbol of their friendship. Gene hesitates, then, "Holding firmly to the trunk, I took a step toward him, and then my knees bent and I jounced the limb." Finny falls from the tree, and lands with a terrible thud. Then Gene moves out to the edge of the limb with "unthinking sureness," and jumps, "every trace of my fear of this forgotten." The climactic event is told in a matter-of-fact voice, adding a chilling tone to the story. Finny has fallen, and with his absence, Gene is suddenly confident and fearless.

The fall occurs early in the story, and underlies the bulk of the narrative. It is the central episode to the novel. The degree of Gene's guilt, and his actual intentions, is never fully resolved. It is impossible to know how much, if any, forethought entered into the moment when Gene caused the limb to jounce. Whether guilty or not, Gene sometimes seems petty and hostile, and he certainly acts guilty; by the end, he must come to terms with his culpability. Gene refuses to explain himself and tell us the information we need; thus, the reader can be fully engaged in the story and often feel sympathetic toward Gene, but also maintain a critical stance.

Critics such as James Ellis have pointed out Knowles's use of Christian symbolism in the novel. The tree is symbolic of the cross, and Finny is the Christ-like figure who must be sacrificed for his sins. The tree also symbolizes the biblical tree of knowledge, "the means by which Gene will renounce the Eden-like summer peace of Devon, and, in so doing, both fall from innocence and at the same time prepare himself for the second world war. As in the fall of Genesis, there is concerning this tree a temptation" (313). The serpent, Gene discovers, is within himself. But Peter Wolfe adds, "Lacking a single meaning, the tree stands for reality itself" (192). Then, reality has toppled Finny; he has fallen to earth.

5

Finny's fall represents the end of the magical summer and boyhood innocence. The illusion of peace has deserted Devon. Finny's shattered leg has affected the entire campus, even the masters. "It was as though they felt it was especially unfair that it should strike one of the 16 year olds, one of the few young men who could be free and happy in the summer of 1942."

Nobody suspects Gene of any wrongdoing, but he feels guilty and listless. "I spent as much time as I could alone in our room, trying to empty my mind of every thought, to forget where I was, even who I was." Gene's inability to know himself is one of the major themes in the novel. Finny clearly has the stronger personality, so that Gene is unsure who he is; while this fall has made a cripple of Finny, it has subjected Gene to a new perception of himself in relation to Finny.

Though their personalities contrast each other, in other ways, Finny and Gene seem like twins. Physically, they are the same height and nearly the same weight; they share clothes and spend most of their time together. With Finny gone, Gene now seems drawn to fill his void. He puts on Finny's clothes, including his pink shirt: "I was Phineas, Phineas to the life." Gene's jealousy of Finny culminates with his desire to want to be him. He explains, "I had no idea why this gave me such intense relief, but it seemed, standing there in Finny's triumphant shirt, that I would never stumble through the confusion of my own character again." If Gene can "be" Finny, then he too will be confident, good, and "noble." Gene's insecurities dominate his perceptions about himself. By blurring the line between his own identity and Finny's, Gene can relieve himself of guilt, escaping from his own self by wearing another's clothes. Gene does not have to face the darkness in his own heart because he can embody Finny: "The sense of transformation stayed with me throughout the evening, and even when I undressed and went to bed."

Yet Gene's transformation disappears in the morning, and his guilt returns even more intensely when Dr. Stanpole tells him that Finny will be able to walk but that sports are finished for him. In a moment of vulnerability, Gene breaks down: "I burst out crying into my hands; I cried for Phineas and for myself and for this doctor who believed in facing things. Most of all I cried because of kindness, which I had not expected." This kindness of the doctor, and also Gene's concern for Finny, surprises him, as juxtaposed to his darker side.

Dr. Stanpole tells Gene that he must be strong for Finny. Gene fears that Finny will accuse him of his crime when they meet face to face, and his way to handle this is to react with lies and feigned disbelief. When he approaches Finny in the infirmary, he asks, "What happened, what happened? How did you fall, how could you fall off like that?" He feels that Finny's eyes were "vaguely on my face," as Finny explains that "something jiggled." Then Finny adds, "it was like I had all the time in the world, I thought I could reach and get hold of you."

Gene reacts to these words by flinching violently away from Finny. Perhaps he is afraid that Finny knows the truth. His first impulse is to lie, by telling Finny that he tried to reach for him. Finny responds, "I just remember looking at your face for a second. Awfully funny expression you had. Very shocked, like you have right now." Finny's observation lets the reader see Gene's fear and guilt. When Gene asks Finny if he remembers what made him fall, Finny responds, "I had a kind of feeling. But you can't say anything for sure from just feelings." It is possible then that Finny suspects the truth, but refuses to accept this about his friend, and he even apologizes for having the thought. In this moment, Gene knows that "he was never going to accuse me." And again, Gene sees Finny as superior. "And I thought we were competitors! It was so ludicrous. I wanted to cry." Gene explains that he is on the verge of telling the truth, but then Dr. Stanpole enters, and Gene leaves without confessing.

Gene goes home to see his family, to somewhere in the south where he is from (he never says exactly where). Nothing is revealed about this visit. Then at the end of September, 1942, he returns to Devon for the next session. On the way, he stops by Finny's house. Finny, happy to see him, is talkative and friendly, until Gene finally confesses:

"I deliberately jounced the limb so you would fall off." He looked older than I had ever seen him. "Of course you didn't."

"Yes I did. I did!"

"Of course you didn't do it. You damn fool. Sit down, you damn fool."

"Of course I did!"

Finny is furious. His affection and loyalty for Gene does not allow him to believe that Gene could hurt him. But how much does Finny know, and how much will his own denial hurt him in the end? Finny tells Gene he'll kill him if he doesn't shut up, and then Gene realizes,

I was injuring him again. It occurred to me that this could be an even deeper injury than what I had done before. I would have to back out of it, I would have to disown it. Could it be that he might even be right? . . . I couldn't remember, I couldn't think. However it was, it was worse for him to know it.

The only way for Gene to move on is to be forgiven by Finny, or sever the friendship and to let himself forget. But Finny's adamant denial and his desire to cling to the relationship does not allow Gene to free himself.

6

The Devon School 1942–1943 winter term starts in Chapter 6, as the teachers try to return the school to its proper austere atmosphere: "Devon had slipped through their fingers during the warm overlooked months. The traditions had been broken, the standards let down, all rules forgotten." Gene misses the summer, the "wayward gypsy music, leading us down all kinds of foolish gypsy ways, unforgiving. I was glad of it, I had almost caught the rhythm of it, the dancing, clicking jangle of it during the summer." Gene wishes he could have "caught the rhythm," like Finny, but the reader knows that Gene's light summer was also tainted by jealousy. Still, Gene clings to the idea of summer as a gentle time which "had come to an end, in the last long rays of daylight at the tree, when Phineas fell."

In the previous chapters, the war remains mostly in the background, but now, in the winter chapters, the war takes on increased significance, as it is becoming more of a reality for the boys. The school is now back in the hands of the masters and students such as Brinker Hadley. The first mention of Brinker Hadley occurs in Chapter 6, "the trays of snails which Leper had passed the summer collecting replaced by Brinker's files." The summer, ruled by Finny, is contrasted to Brinker, the ruler of winter, with "his steady with and ceaseless plans."

Knowles develops mood and plot by the use of contrasting symbols—winter versus summer, as well as the two rivers that Devon sits astride. The Devon River is a freshwater river, the one into which Finny and Gene jumped from the tree. This river symbolizes summer, "where we'd had so much fun." Even now, Gene feels at peace when he looks at the Devon River:

> As I had to do whenever I glimpsed this river, I thought of Phineas. Not of the tree and pain, but of one of his favorite tricks, Phineas in exaltation, balancing on one foot on the prow of a canoe like a river god, his raised arms invoking the air to support him, face transfigured, body a complex set of balances and compensations, each muscle alighted in perfection . . .

Gene's comparison of Finny to a river god exemplifies the way he views him, his beauty, godliness, and immortality. It is easier for him to remember Finny like this, and not as the maimed boy he saw at his parents' house. Gene feels more comfortable with this illusion: "I stopped in the middle of this hurrying day to remember him like that, and then, feeling refreshed . . ."

While the Devon River connotes peace, purity, and goodness, in the winter, it is overtaken by the Naguamsett River, the lower river. This river—marshy, salty, and cold—connects with the ocean, and thus, is controlled by global forces, "unimaginable factors like the Gulf Stream, the Polar Ice Cap, and the moon." It is symbolic of the oncoming conflict, explains Mellard: "But as the war overtakes peace, and winter replaces summer, the highland Devon must drop into the lowland Naguamsett, a vicissitude which suggests once again that youth cannot avoid the responsibilities of maturity" (130).

Gene has volunteered to be assistant crew manager, and he shows up for his duties at the crew house, which sits next to the Naguamsett. When Gene arrives, he is confronted by the senior crew manager, Cliff Quackenbush, disliked by the other students, and a bully. Gene goes about his duties and feels Quackenbush observing him to see if he walks with a limp—as usually the boys who volunteer to be managers are disabled—but Gene knows that Quackenbush's "flat black eyes would never detect my trouble." Gene is emotionally maimed, as Finny is physically maimed.

Quackenbush implies that Gene must not be good enough to row if he wants to be a manager, and Gene is put off by Quackenbush's "furious arrogance." Gene's reasons for withdrawing from sports can be read in several contexts. The most obvious is that Gene is aligning himself with Finny, that when Dr. Stanpole said sports are finished, it was as if he was talking to him. On the other hand, withdrawing from sports is also a way for him to separate himself from Finny. Gene also explains a new fear of play and the possibility of violence, relying on war imagery: "as though even a tennis ball might turn into a bullet."

Gene's unfriendly interaction with Quackenbush intensifies his feelings of loss for Finny. His love for Finny, and his desire for innocence and the joy of youth, rushes over him:

> It was only that [Quackenbush] was so ignorant, that he knew nothing of the gypsy summer, nothing of the loss I was fighting to endure, of skylarks and splashes and petal bearing breezes, he had not seen Leper's snails or the Charter of the SSS; he shared nothing, knew nothing, felt nothing as Phineas had done.

It is almost as if Gene now sees himself as Finny, as if the two identities have merged into one; after he thinks of Finny, he tells Quackenbush, "You . . . don't know anything about who I am."

When Quackenbush calls him a "maimed son-of a bitch," Gene hits him and the two get into a fight and fall into the river. Gene believes he's defending Finny, but then admits, "But it didn't feel exactly as though I had done it for Phineas. It felt as though I had done it for myself." If Gene thought he could sever his friendship with Finny, he must realize that now it is impossible. After the fight with Quackenbush, Gene, drenched, goes back to the dorm. Wired with anger, he notices that "one of my legs wouldn't stop trembling, whether from cold or anger I couldn't tell," confusing himself with Finny.

In contrast to Gene's plunge into the Devon River in Chapter 1, now Gene has been baptized in the Naguamsett, symbolizing Gene's fall, and his lost youth: "I stood there shaking in my wet sneakers. If only I had truly taken advantage of the situation, seized and held and prized the multitudes of advantages the summer offered me; if only I had." Instead of basking in the summer lightness, Gene had fallen prey to some darkness within him.

Back at the dorm, there is a phone message, and the number "which seemed to interrupt the beating of my heart" is Finny's. Gene returns the call and everything is light again: "Friendliness, simple outgoing affection, that was all I could hear in his voice." Finny wants to make sure that Gene is no longer "crazy," the way he was on his last visit, when he tried to confess.

Finny is horrified to find out that Gene is not playing sports. His influence over Gene is palpable: "Listen, pal, if I can't play sports, you're going to play them for me." Gene at this moment lets go of any attempt to distance himself from Finny. Gene cannot yet be his own person, and Finny encourages Gene to fill his place. Gene admits, "I lost part of myself to him then, and a soaring sense of freedom revealed that this must have been my purpose from the first: to become a part of Phineas." After speaking to Finny, Gene washes off the Naguamsett River, but symbolically, he cannot wash away his guilt; he experienced his own fall the day that Finny hurtled from the tree.

Brinker Hadley makes his first appearance in Chapter 7, and will become one the novel's main characters. Brinker, the opposite of Finny, represents rules and order, even "his face was all straight lines." Brinker is a class leader, active in school committees and well-liked by the other students. In contrast to Finny and the gypsy summer, Brinker is associated with "Winter Session efficiency."

Chapter 7 begins to foreshadow the trial in Chapter 11, in which Brinker hopes to discover the truth of Finny's fall. Brinker is the first to suspect Gene, and the one most adamant about finding out the truth. Now, Brinker jokingly accuses Gene of getting rid of Finny on purpose so that he could have his room to himself. "The truth hurts, eh?" Gene tries to keep up with the humorous tone, but realizes that his "voice sounded too strained even to my own blood-pounded ears."

The boys go down to the Butt Room, "something like a dungeon," where the students hang out and smoke. Brinker continues to push Gene, joking that he did "away with his roommate," and Gene knows that he must participate, in order not to look guilty. He jokes about planning an elaborate plan to kill Finny, but chokes and cannot say, "I pushed him out of the tree." Instead, he turns on a younger boy in the room, directing attention away from himself and ridiculing the boy. Gene leaves the room without a smoke, which others notice, but "this was a clue they soon seemed to forget."

After a snow storm, the Devon students, including Gene, Brinker, Quackenbush, and Chet Douglass, shovel snow from the railroad yards, in order to relieve the wartime labor shortage. While the boys are shoveling snow, a troop train goes by, the soldiers "not much older than we were." Although the significance of the war is growing in the novel, it still has very little direct effect on the boys, as represented in the poem that Brinker Hadley composes, "The War/Is a Bore." The boys are caught in limbo, a state of purgatory, as they wait to join the war—it is their future, but there is nothing to do about it now. One day they will be a part of the war, but now they are safe at school, in a separate peace; the tension of waiting wears them down.

While the other boys shovel snow, Leper Lepellier, an introverted biology student, who "made little sketches of birds and trees in the back of his notebook during chapel," goes skiing, on the search for beaver dams: "I just like to go along and see what I'm passing and enjoy myself." Leper has not yet fallen from grace or the spell of the summer. Dreamy and romantic, Leper is the opposite of Brinker Hadley, who does not try to hide his disdain for Leper.

After a conversation with Leper, Gene and Brinker walk off, and Brinker tells Gene that he is going to enlist, in order to put an end to the waiting. Gene admits, "I felt a thrill when he said it." To enlist would be the surest way for Gene to leave his old life, a way to sever himself from his guilt:

To enlist. To slam the door impulsively on the past, to shed everything down to my last bit of clothing, to break the pattern of my life—that complex design I had been weaving since birth with all its dark threads, its unexplainable symbols set against a conventional background of domestic white and schoolboy blue, all those tangled strands which required the dexterity of a virtuoso to keep flowing. . .

Gene decides that he will enlist too. Happy with his decision, he bounds up the stairs, and there, sitting at the desk, is Finny, his link to the past and the one who still influences Gene's every move. Finny's presence easily overpowers his idea to enlist: "Everything that had happened throughout the day faded like that first false snowfall of the winter. Phineas was back."

7

In Chapter 8, Gene realizes that he and Finny have grown apart on their views on the war. After Finny complains about the loss of the maid services, Gene "felt a certain disproval of him for grumbling about a lost luxury, with a war on." Finny chooses to live in a world of illusion—he ignores the war, trusts Gene would never hurt him, and rarely acknowledges his leg. Gene draws a line between his own views and Finny's:

Until now, in spite of everything, I had welcomed each new day as though it were a new life, where all past failures and problems were erased, and all future possibilities and joys open and available, to be achieved probably before night fell again. Now, in this winter of snow and crutches with Phineas, I began to know that each morning reasserted the problems of the night before, that sleep suspended all but changed nothing, that you couldn't make yourself over between dawn and dusk. Phineas however did not believe this.

Despite the constant reminder of his maimed leg, Finny needs to hold onto the belief that there are no problems. "In Finny's universe all things are possible as long as the bulwark of illusion holds; as long as Finny can believe each morning, for example, that his leg has miraculously healed, there is evidence for all magic, not only his but that of a sympathetic universe," attests Witherington (799).

One day Brinker comes in to talk to Gene about enlisting, and Finny is surprised and hurt: "His large and clear eyes turned with an odd expression on me. I had never seen such a look in them before." In the same way that Gene seems to define himself through Finny, Finny seems unprepared to live his life without Gene:

> . . . Phineas was shocked at the idea of my leaving. In some way he needed me. He needed me. I was the least trustworthy person he had ever met. I knew that; he knew or should know that too. I had even told him. I had told him. . . . He wanted me around. The war then passed away from me, and dreams of enlistment and escape and a clean start lost their meaning for me.

For Gene, there is no escape, no chance to sever the relationship; he cannot let go of their friendship or the charade that nothing is wrong. To please Finny, he turns the idea of enlisting into a joke, and Finny's face broke "into a wide and dazzled smile at what I had said, lighting up his whole face." Though Brinker still talks about enlisting, he will not do it alone.

For a while, it seems possible that Gene and Finny can go back to the way things were. Finny's fall has not driven a wedge between them, but instead has tightened the bond. With the return of Finny, it as if the peace of summer has returned: ". . . For the war was no longer eroding the peaceful summertime stillness I had prized so much at Devon." The atmosphere slowly gives way to Finny's world, of play and innocence. Though the reality of winter is everywhere, the playing fields "crusted under a foot of congealed snow and the river was now a hard gray-white lane of ice between gaunt trees," for Gene, "peace had come back to Devon for me." The war almost took Gene, swept him up in its wave, until Finny returned and Gene "ducked," so that now he is "peaceably treading water as before."

Even the harsh winter, with its icy patches that make it difficult to maneuver on crutches, does not faze Finny. He tells Gene he likes winter and that it likes him, explaining, "when you really love something, then it loves you back." The line captures Finny's feelings for Gene—he loves Gene, so he naturally expects that Gene feels the same. Gene knows, from his own experience, that this is not true, though "it was like every other thought and belief of Finny's . . . it should have been true."

Despite Finny's insistence on the winter's love, Knowles draws a sharp contrast between the gypsy days of summer and the winter's snow and ice, which make it difficult for Finny to get around. Now he "picked his way with surprising care," contrasted to before the fall, when he moved in "continuous flowing balancing, so that he had seemed to drift along with no effort at all, relaxation on the move." Now, he "hobbled." Though Finny tries to ignore his shattered leg, it is always with him: "Phineas was a poor deceiver, having had no practice."

One day, Finny decides he wants to go to the gym, which is described in reverent language, almost like a church, with the "marble archway, glisteningly white, which led to the pool." The boys enter the locker room, and Gene describes the odor as one with "meaning and poignancy for any athlete, just as it has for any lover."

Since Finny can no longer play sports, he decides that Gene is "going to be the big star now." Finny now looks at Gene as an extension of himself. Critic Peter Wolfe points out, "Ironically, Finny is just as eager as Gene to switch identities. Rather than accusing him of treachery or languishing in self-pity, he tries to recover some of his lost splendor through his friend" (194).

At first, Gene resists, telling Finny that sports do not seem as important now, with the war. Finny responds, "Have you swallowed all that war stuff?" He tells Gene that there isn't any war. According to Finny, the war is a conspiracy orchestrated by fat old men who are making money off the fantasy: "They've made it all up." Finny's injury has placed him in a "separate peace." While his friends will go to war, he will not because he is crippled, and he does not want to be isolated or alienated from his friends, especially from Gene; thus, if he cannot be a part of the war, then he cannot let it exist. Finny's general belief that the world is good parallels his feelings about Gene; he cannot accept that Gene feels any resentment or dark feelings toward him: "The reality of war is lost upon him because he is constitutionally pure and incapable of malice" (Ellis 314).

Gene, however, does not abandon reality so easily: "For a moment I was almost taken in by it. Then my eyes fell on the bound and cast white mass pointing at me, and as it was always to do, it brought me down out of Finny's world of invention . . . down to reality, to the facts." The cast is a constant reminder of Finny's fall from the tree, and Gene's fall from innocence. Then Gene asks Finny how only he knows that the war is a hoax. "His face froze. 'Because I've suffered,' he burst out." His honest answer surprises both boys. Gene sees that Phineas "had been even more startled than I to discover this bitterness in himself." This is a rare moment in which Finny acknowledges the reality of his situation, where his guard is let down and the fantasy crumbles.

There is an awkward silence. In order to downplay the tension, Gene approaches the exercise bar and "in a fumbling and perhaps grotesque offering to Phineas, I chinned myself.

I couldn't think of anything else, not the right words, not the right gesture. I did what I could think of." Finny recovers and orders Gene to do 30 chin-ups. Sports continue to be the "absolute good" for Finny, a way to preserve peace and youth.

Finny decides that he is going to train Gene for the 1944 Olympics. He reasons that since he always wanted to be an Olympic athlete, now Gene will take his place, contributing to the merging of identities. When Gene tries to argue that there won't be any Olympics because of the war, Finny responds "Leave your fantasy life out of this." Gene does not argue: "And not believing him, not forgetting that troops were being shuttled toward battlefields all over the world, I went along, as I always did, with any new invention of Finny's."

Time passes. Finny trains Gene for the Olympics, while Gene tutors Finny. It seems possible that they may discover a healthy balance. Then one morning, on a long training run, Gene finds his rhythm. Finny, cheering him on, tells Gene, "You didn't even know anything about yourself." Finny sees himself as Gene's mirror. But while Gene has been defining himself through Finny, on this day, he feels different. He notices that Finny "seemed older that morning, and leaning quietly against that great tree wrapped in his heavy coat, he seemed smaller too. Or perhaps it was only that I inside the same body, had felt myself all at once grown bigger." Gene, then, is growing, whereas Finny is slowly fading: "At first he thinks of himself, rather guiltily, as an extension of Finny, but after becoming an athlete in his own right he sees Finny as smaller, both relatively and absolutely, like memories from childhood . . ." (Witherington 800).

When Mr. Ludsbury comes over to ask them what they're doing, Finny tells him about the Olympics, and the stern teacher warns them that everything they do should be in preparation for the war. Finny says, "No," flustering his teacher. This is the first time in which Finny responds without his typical charm; he will not allow his illusion to be challenged.

Finny's love for games and play is fully realized with the Winter Carnival in Chapter 9. Gene allows himself to be swept away by Finny's illusion: "What deceived me was my own happiness; for peace is indivisible, and the surrounding world confusion found no reflection inside me. So I ceased to have any real sense of it."

Even when dreamy, peaceful Leper enlists, the war does not seem any more real to Gene or the other boys, who have no way to imagine Leper, with his "snails and beaver dams" entering a world of violence. Leper decided to enlist after he saw a recruitment film of the ski troops. "To Leper it revealed what all of us were seeking; a recognizable and friendly face to the war." Gene has no such connection: "How did it apply to me, and to Phineas?"

After a while, down in the Butt Room, the boys begin to accept that Leper has enlisted by making jokes about him, connecting headlines to Leper, so that he is behind every Allied victory. Finny is the only one who doesn't participate in these jokes, which would mean admitting that the war is real. Instead, he brings Gene into his private world: "He drew me increasingly away from the Butt Room crowd, away from Brinker and Chet and all other friends, into a world inhabited by just himself and me, where there was no war at all, just Phineas and me alone among all the people of the world, training for the Olympics of 1944." Finny has created a separate peace for him and Gene. Critics have questioned whether Finny is as innocent as he appears, or if his innocence equals goodness. "There is something almost diabolical about Finny's 'innocence.' His power over people is uncanny," suggests Witherington. "Gene describes it as hypnotic, and it consists of enticing others temporarily to suspend their practical, logical systems of belief to follow his non-logical argument, acted out either verbally or on the playing fields" (796).

Finny decides to break up the monotony of winter with a carnival, assigning tasks to the boys, including the creation of a ski jump and snow statues. The Winter Carnival represents the climactic battle for the summer to prevail over the winter, and models a Dionysian festival, in which the Greeks celebrated Dionysus, the god of drink and pleasure. Critic Marvin E. Mengeling points out, "Knowles surely bore in mind the festival of Dionysus when erecting his superb carnival scene.

In a sense, this invention of Phineas marks his resurrection" (1327). For the festival, all rules and order are abandoned, and Gene observes, "There was going to be no government, even by whim, even by Brinker's whim, on this Saturday at Devon." Brinker has become more disillusioned with school organizations and activities, "his well-bred clothes had disappeared; these days he wore khaki pants supported by a garrison belt, and boots which rattled when he walked," but he still has faith in rules and order. At the carnival, he guards the hard cider, and tries to get the games to proceed in an orderly fashion. However, in a moment of unhinged chaos, encouraged by Finny, the other boys attack Brinker. Brinker is unable to stand up to Finny and his anarchic force, and the summer session easily overpowers the winter.

In addition to the allusion to Dionysus, there are many other references to the Greek games throughout the chapter. Finny, the unofficial leader, opens the festival with fire, symbolically setting fire to *The Iliad*, Homer's book of war, while Gene "must act as the Chorus." At the end, Finny orders "Olympic candidate" Gene Forrester to qualify for the decathlon, and Gene performs a number of athletic feats, surprising even himself. He is then crowned by Finny; as Finny predicted, Gene has become the star athlete, taking on Finny's role.

On this last attempt to hold onto the summer, the boys are drunk on cider and life itself, especially Finny, who performs a wild graceful dance on one leg on the table:

> Under the influence not I know of the hardest cider but of his own inner joy at life for a moment as it should be, as it was meant to be in his nature, Phineas recaptured that magic gift for existing primarily in space, one foot conceding briefly to gravity its rights before spinning him off again into the air. It was his widest demonstration of himself, of himself in the kind of world he loved; it was his choreography of peace.

Phineas succeeds in creating a world of peace and innocence, a "liberation we had torn from the gray encroachments of 1943, the escape we had concocted, this afternoon of momentary, illusory, special and separate peace." Yet, as Gene discovers, his innocence and peace do not endure.

The carnival is cut short by the arrival of a telegram from Leper, addressed to Gene, symbolic of how the war interrupts the boys' youth and innocence. The telegram explains that Leper has "escaped" from the army, and he wants Gene to meet him, signing the telegram, "Your best friend." This line surprises the reader—is Leper deluding himself? Or is there an area of Gene's life that he neglected or simply refuses to illuminate for the reader?

8

Gene's visit to Vermont to see Leper unfolds in Chapter 10. The novel has taken a dark turn; the reality of war can no longer be ignored. Eden, represented by the summer, cannot exist in a world with war, and now the setting is cold and dreary, a place where, "the natural state of things is coldness, and houses are fragile havens, holdouts in a death landscape."

Leper rises as a major character, first for enlisting and then for deserting. Gene meets with Leper at his parents' house and soon Gene realizes that Leper has unraveled. Leper's mental breakdown parallels Finny's physical breakdown; of the Devon students, Leper and Finny are the first two causalities of the war, destroyed because of their innocence and refusal to look at reality.

The army was planning to give Leper a Section 8 discharge, for insanity, and so he ran away. Gene now sees the reality of what the war can do to a boy, and he selfishly admits that he is more concerned about himself: "it was myself I was worried about. For if Leper was psycho it was the army which had done it to him, and I and all of us were on the brink of the army." Leper represents the other side, the loss of youth; he has seen the face of the war.

In this crucial scene, Leper tells Gene that he was at the tree that night and accuses him of knocking Finny out of the tree, "that time you crippled him for life," bringing Gene's fears out into the open. Leper says, "You always were a savage underneath," and Gene reacts by kicking Leper's chair over. He cannot stand to hear Leper's words, realizing that Leper has seen the darkness inside of him. The critic James L. McDonald points to this scene as an example of how Gene is an unreliable narrator: "The reader's awareness of this discrepancy is enforced by the dramatic statements of other characters in the novel, especially by the comments of Leper" (336). Leper has referred to himself as Gene's best friend, and now describes Gene as vengeful: "You always were a lord of the manor, weren't you? A swell guy, except when the chips were down." The reader is being given new information about Gene, but is not certain how to put it all together, since Gene is not forthcoming about these parts of his life.

Gene and Leper go on a walk, the setting symbolizes the dark atmosphere of the novel: "We roamed across one of these wastes, our feet breaking through at each step the thin surface crust of ice into a layer of soft snow underneath." It feels very far from Devon's separate peace. The war has broken Leper, who suffers from terrible hallucinations. When he describes them to Gene, he tells him to stop: "I didn't want to hear any more of it. Not now or ever. I didn't care because it had nothing to do with me. And I didn't want to hear any more of it. Ever." Gene finally runs off into the snowy fields, leaving Leper by himself: "Gene's failure is one of moral escapism. When Leper reveals himself as a misfit in a world where nothing fits with anything else Gene flees. Leper's description of the ugliness and disjointedness underlying life strikes Gene so hard that he must deny it in order to keep peace with himself" (Wolfe 197).

Chapter 11 parallels Chapter 4, in that Finny will fall a second time. The chapter begins with Gene, returning to Devon after his trip to see Leper: "I wanted to see Phineas, and Phineas only." When Gene returns, he finds Finny engaged in a snowball fight, "playing and fighting—the two were approximately the same thing to him." For Finny, fighting is always a form of play, without violence, competition, or jealousy. The snowball fight defines Finny, his love for pure sport, with no winners or losers.

Gene stops at the edge of the snowball game, "too tangled in my mind to enter either one or the other." Now Gene knows he cannot look away from reality, that he is the one who caused Finny's fall, but he cannot yet completely sever himself from the illusion of peace. Finny draws him in the snowball fight, and he is "engulfed." The boys "ended the fight the only way possible; all of us turned on Phineas. Slowly, with a steadily widening grin, he was driven down beneath a blizzard of snowballs." This innocent game foreshadows how Finny will be brought down by his friends. It also reveals that Finny's illusion cannot prevail, that it will topple.

> For Finny, life is a continuous effort to control reality by creating comfortable myths about it. War is only make-believe on the field and rivers of Devon: a game resembling football and soccer is invented and named, for its speed and devastating unpredictability, 'blitzball;' snowball fights are staged as military operations; the tree hanging over the Devon River is a torpedoed ship that must be evacuated. But these games which at first seem to have the practical function of preparing boys mentally and physically for war actually become shields against reality, ways of sugarcoating the externals of war by making its participants invulnerable. (Witherington, 798).

Now the war is hurdling toward the boys, destroying any illusions of innocence.

Still, Gene tries to keep up the fantasy, for Finny's sake. Joking, he emphasizes that there is no war, but Finny destroys the fantasy with his tone of irony: "his grin flashed and faded, then he murmured, 'Sure. There isn't any war.' Gene observes, "It was one of the few ironic remarks Phineas ever made, and with it he quietly brought to a close all his special inventions which had carried us through the winter. Now the facts were re-established, and gone were all the fantasies, such as the Olympic Games for 1944, closed before they had ever been opened." Leper's breakdown marks the end of the boys' games, even for Finny. This scene also reveals that Finny has lost some of his vibrant youth, showing hints of cynicism.

In Chapter 10 Knowles provides a description of Finny and Gene's room for the first time. Gene, from the south, mentions that there are pictures of a plantation mansion over his cot, which amounted to "a barefaced lie about my background." Gene has tried to construct a false identity for himself, a detail the reader learns late in the novel. "When asked about [the pictures] I had acquired an accent appropriate to a town three states south of my own, and I had transmitted the impression, without actually stating it, that this was the old family place." This passage highlights Gene's unreliability; we as readers become more suspicious of him. Yet, in the same passage, Gene claims that he does not need those pictures anymore, that he is finding himself. "But by now I no longer need this vivid false identity; now I was acquiring, I felt, a sense of my own real authority and worth, I had had many new experiences and I was growing up."

One day, Brinker takes Gene aside and accuses him of pitying Finny. Brinker says that Finny needs to accept the truth of his leg, that nobody ever mentions it except for Brinker. As the argument escalates, Brinker says, "You've got a little personal stake in this. What I mean is it wouldn't do you any harm, you know, if everything about Finny's accident was cleared up and forgotten." The taunting comment suggests that Brinker believes that Gene knows more about Finny's fall than he's letting on.

Time passes. All of the boys, except Gene, take steps toward enlisting. The tension is building, the war becoming more of a reality, even for Finny. He admits to Gene, "When I heard that about Leper, then I knew that the war was real, this war and all the wars. If a war can drive somebody crazy, then it's real all right. Oh I guess I always *knew*, but I didn't want to have to admit it." Finny believes in Leper's breakdown because he actually saw Leper. This is an important plot point: Leper is on campus. Gene is surprised by this, but they decide not to tell anyone.

The calm between Gene and Finny does not last. That night, Brinker and his cohorts burst into the room and take

Finny and Gene to the Assembly Hall, where above the door, in Latin, is the phrase, "Here Boys Come to Be Made Men." The room resembles a courtroom. Brinker, who believes that the truth must be discovered no matter what the cost, presides over the makeshift tribunal. Other boys serve as the audience and as a panel of judges, dressed in black graduation robes. Gene, worried, wants to believe that Brinker is playing a joke, but "There was nothing funny about the Assembly Room."

The games and the playing have gone too far, but Gene realizes they missed the moment to stop this, that now there is no turning back. Brinker orders Finny to tell them what happened when he fell out of the tree. At first, Finny tries to ignore Brinker, speaking "in a constricted voice." Then Finny lies. He says that Gene was at the bottom of the tree. But as he continues, seeming to convince himself with these made up details, he suddenly remembers that he'd suggested a double-jump and he cracks. He realizes that they must have climbed the tree together. Gene struggles to defend the discrepancy between his and Finny's stories. At this point, the reader is unsure if Finny knows of Gene's cruelty. Is he oblivious, or does he know everything and chose to see only what he wants to?

Brinker laments that if Leper were around, he could clear the whole thing up. Gene watches Finny:

Phineas had been sitting motionless, leaning slightly forward, not far from the position in which we prayed at Devon. After a long time he turned and reluctantly looked at me. I did not return his look or move or speak. Then at last Finny straightened from this prayerful position slowly, as though it was painful for him. "Leper's here," he said.

By revealing that Leper is on campus, Finny sets the truth in motion.

A few of the boys go to find Leper, then he takes the stand. He gives a descriptive, poetic image of what he saw that day, the two figures looked "as black as death standing up there with this fire burning all around them." Leper is strangely confident and composed, but Gene reminds himself that Leper is crazy and rationalizes that no one will believe him: "Everyone could hear, couldn't they? The derangement in his voice." Because of the earlier scene with Gene, it is unclear to the reader as to Leper's motivations. Is he simply there to describe what he witnessed, or is he taking revenge?

Leper describes the two figures on the tree as moving "like an engine." In this dramatic moment, Gene realizes that there is no more pretending: "In the baffled silence I began to uncoil slowly." Leper continues, "in this engine first one piston sinks, and then the next one sinks. The one holding onto the trunk sank for a second, up and down like a piston, and then the other one sank and fell." Leper will not say which of them fell; he suddenly clams up, suspicious of Brinker's intentions. Gene refuses to show his emotions, but Phineas has heard enough. He gets out of his seat and says, "I don't care." Gene stands up and calls after him, but, "He shook his head sharply, closing his eyes, and then he turned to regard me with a handsome mask of a face. 'I just don't care. Never mind . . .'" When Brinker tells him not to go, "We haven't got all the facts!" Finny breaks down. Crying, he plunges out the doors, and then the boys hear the terrible crash.

9

Chapter 12 begins in the moments following Finny's fall down the marble staircase. The boys take the necessary steps—someone runs to get Dr. Stanpole, and others rush to bring Phil Latham, the wrestling coach. Gene notices that Phil Latham wraps a blanket around Phineas, and he thinks "I would have liked very much to have done that myself; it would have meant a lot to me."

Gene is scared, but he feels reassured by Dr. Stanpole's words that it is a simple fracture "a much cleaner break." To find out more about what's going on, Gene sneaks into the infirmary, and when Finny sees him, for the first time, his rage is unleashed. He yells, "You want to break something else in me! Is that why you're here!" Gene responds, "I'm sorry . . . I'm sorry, I'm sorry."

Gene then leaves Finny and blindly walks around campus; he feels like he can see a new level of meaning in everything around him. His nighttime wandering leads him to a tragic realization that he has no sense of self or identity. ". . . and I alone was a dream, a figment which had never really touched anything. I felt that I was not, never had been and never would be a living part of this overwhelmingly solid and deeply meaningful world around me." Gene spent so much of the novel losing himself to Finny, that now that he is severed from him, he feels himself to be a ghost: "But I could not hear, and that was because I did not exist."

When Gene wakes up the next morning, he no longer feels separate from the world. He will face the truth of what happened; he will face himself. Finny was a victim of his own innocence, contrasted to Gene, who in the face of evil, gains self-knowledge.

Dr. Stanpole leaves Gene a note to bring some of Finny's things to the infirmary. Gene packs a suitcase and returns to the infirmary, unsure what to say to Phineas, but ready to face him. "I couldn't escape a confusing sense of having lived through this all before . . . I seemed to be less shocked by it now than I had the first time last August." This time, when Finny sees him, he seems nervous, his hand shaking. Gene reminds him that he had tried to tell him the truth once before, at his house, and Finny answers, "I know, I remember that." When Finny asks Gene why he came, Gene says he had to: "I thought I belonged here."

In anger and frustration, Finny slams his fist on the suitcase, and bursts out, "I wish to God there wasn't any war." If there were no war, in Finny's view, then he would not have had to face his best friend's betrayal, and in a larger sense, the fall of man. But the war can no longer be ignored. As the novel progresses in time, the images from the magazines and newsreels have grown more horrible, and although at first the boys seem to be protected, the war is already within the walls of Devon, already within them. "We members of the Class of 1943 were moving very fast toward the war now, so fast that there were causalities even before we reached it, a mind was clouded and a leg was broken."

Finny then reveals to Gene something he doesn't know—that Finny spent the winter writing to various military branches all over the Allied world, begging to let him enlist, but was rejected because of his leg. He says the reason he kept saying there was no war was because he could not be a part of it, another example of his refusal to look outside of himself. This moment shows the reader that there may be more to Finny than Gene has realized, that he is not a simple symbol of innocence or naiveté. Then Gene tells him, "Phineas, you wouldn't be any good in the war, even if nothing had happened to your leg." He goes on to say that Finny would make a mess of the war—he would have gone to the other side and made friends and gotten everyone confused about who they were fighting. Though Gene is joking, he realizes this is also the truth: Finny cannot survive a war, he cannot survive a fallen world.

Finny bursts into tears. The second fall has forced Finny to acknowledge something blind in man's character; if he does not accept this idea of blind evil, then he must admit that Gene wanted to hurt him on purpose. He addresses Gene, "It was just some kind of blind impulse you had in the tree there, you didn't know what you were doing." He asks Gene to confirm that it was this blind impulse and not some deep harbored feeling against Finny. The reader is never certain if Finny really believes this, or if he is simply forcing himself to believe.

Gene agrees, "It was just some ignorance inside me, some crazy thing inside me, something blind, that's all." According to Ellis, "Gene has discovered that his private evil, which caused him to hurt Phineas, is the same evil—only magnified—that results in war" (318). But was it blind impulse, or malice that had been building up in Gene? The reader is also not certain if Gene believes what he is saying—he tells the reader what he says to Finny, but does not tell us what he is thinking. Finny, however, assures Gene that he believes him. A resolution is reached, a peace between them. Critic Gordon E. Slethaug suggests,

When he comes to the painful awareness that Gene wanted to hurt him, he almost despairs, but Gene's confession to him brings him around once again to an acceptance of their friendship and life, to his belief in the continuing beneficence of their game and friendship. Finny can come to this acceptance because he himself bears no guilt. (267).

Gene's confession leads to the novel's resolution, and freedom comes after his honesty and Finny's acceptance.

Dr. Stanpole tells Gene that he is going to set the bone that afternoon, and to come back that night, when Finny wakes up from the anesthesia. Gene goes about his day mechanically. When he returns, Dr. Stanpole tells him that Finny is dead. "This is something I think boys of your generation are going to see a lot of . . . and I will have to tell you about it now." He explains that bone marrow got in his blood stream and traveled to his heart and killed him. When Gene hears the news, he does not cry, nor does he cry at Finny's funeral. "I could not escape a feeling that his was my own funeral, and you do not cry in that case." This funeral feels like his own because a part of his identity has merged with Finny's, and also because Finny's death represents the death of youth and innocence. The war has fully descended upon Devon: there is no shield or protection. The illusion of immortality is shattered.

Knowles's use of Christian images throughout symbolizes Gene's fall from his innocence, his deliverance and redemption. The novel is an allegory for the concepts of original sin and the fall, according to Mellard, so that "Phineas becomes both Adam and Christ" (131). Finny dies in order to make a sacrifice, so Gene is able to take the next step. According to critic Marvin E. Mengeling, "Physically, Phineas dies. The reasons are twofold. All gods must die physically; it is in their nature to be spiritual, and in the case of many, sacrificial. Phineas dies that Gene might live. Second, Phineas must be crushed physically to emphasize that the present world is really no place for the full blown powers and principles which he represents in his symbolic guise of Phoebus Apollo" (1328).

10

In chapter 13, the concluding chapter, the school year draws to a close, and the war continues, getting closer and closer to Devon. The school has donated the Far Common quadrangle to the military for a parachute riggers school, and soon military trucks and jeeps invade the campus, bringing boyish-looking soldiers and sewing machines, which will be used to make the parachutes, alluding "to the novel's central metaphor of falling . . . the young soldiers will plunge headlong into violence in the same way as Devon's class of 1943" (Wolfe 198). Finny, of course, has already fallen to earth.

In this last chapter, Brinker's father, Mr. Hadley appears, representing the war enthusiasts. Mr. Hadley, a World War I veteran, is upset by the sewing machines, which he sees as weak and effeminate, just as he is disturbed that his son wants to join the Coast Guard and Gene is joining the Navy, in an attempt to stay out of the line of fire. Brinker is resentful toward his father, who talks about the importance of war memories. Later, Brinker denounces his father as part of the older generation causing the war and expecting the younger generation to fight it. Mr. Hadley seems living proof of Finny's theory that the war is nothing but a ruse orchestrated by old men who are fearful of losing their power to the younger generation. However, Gene no longer buys into any of these excuses or explanations for war, as he realizes "that wars were made instead by something ignorant in the human heart."

By the end, the boys lose their childhood illusion that the world is fundamentally a good place. But Finny, until the end, remained untouched, "nothing even about the war had broken his harmonious and natural unity. So at last I had." Gene accepts that he was the one who broke Finny, and now is no longer controlled by fear or hostility. "I was ready for the war, now that I no longer had any hatred to contribute to it. My fury was gone, I felt it gone, dried up at the source, withered and lifeless. Phineas had absorbed it and taken it with him, and I was rid of it forever."

Gene speaks again as an adult. In the army he "never killed anyone or had a deep hatred of the enemy. Because my war ended before I ever put on a uniform; I was on active duty all my time at school; I killed my enemy there." Finny did not believe he had any enemies, which contributed to his tragic fall: he could not comprehend that his best friend would hurt him. Gene admires Finny's views. While all others find something in the world that was against them, a hostile thing, "Phineas alone had escaped this. He possessed an extra vigor, a heightened confidence in himself..." He continues, "Only Phineas never was afraid, only Phineas never hated anyone." After confronting his own fear and hatred, Gene has finally let go of these emotions and has reached a profound understanding about himself and humanity, realizing

> that this enemy never comes from without, but always from within. He knows, moreover that, there is no defense to be built, only an acceptance and purification of oneself through love. Such a love did he share with Phineas in a private gypsy summer. And it is because of the purity of this love that he is able to survive his fall from innocence. (Ellis 318).

Gene makes the decision to live with himself and others in the adult world. By facing himself, he seems to have reached a separate peace—he accepts reality, but will not forget Finny's higher ideals of the way the world should be lived.

Works Cited
Ellis, James, "*A Separate Peace*": The Fall from Innocence," *The English Journal* 53, no. 5 (May 1964): pp. 313–318.
McDonald, James L., "The Novels of John Knowles," *The Arizona Quarterly* 23, no. 4 (Winter 1967): pp. 335–342.
Mellard, James M., "Counterpoint and "Double Vision" in *A Separate Peace*," *Studies in Short Fiction* 4, no. 1 (Winter 1966): pp. 127–134.
Mengeling, Marvin E., "*A Separate Peace*: Meaning and Myth," *The English Journal* 58, no. 9 (Dec 1969): pp. 1322–1329.

Slethaug, Gordon E., "The Play of the Double in *A Separate Peace*," *The Canadian Review of American Studies* 15, no. 3 (Fall 1984): pp. 259–270.

Weber, Ronald, "Narrative Method in *A Separate Peace*," *Studies in Short Fiction* 3, no. 1 (Fall 1965): pp. 63–72.

Witherington, Paul, "*A Separate Peace*: A Study in Structural Ambiguity," *The English Journal* 54, no. 9 (Dec 1965): pp. 795–800.

Wolfe, Peter, "The Impact of Knowles's *A Separate Peace*," *The University Review* 36, no. 3 (Spring 1970): 189–198.

Critical Views

JAMES ELLIS ON INNOCENCE AND ENVY

What happens in the novel is that Gene Forrester and Phineas, denying the existence of the Second World War as they enjoy the summer peace of Devon School, move gradually to a realization of an uglier adult world—mirrored in the winter and the Naguamsett River—whose central fact is the war. This moving from innocence to adulthood is contained within three sets of interconnected symbols. These three—summer and winter; the Devon River and the Naguamsett River; and peace and war—serve as a backdrop against which the novel is developed, the first of each pair dominating the early novel and giving way to the second only after Gene has discovered the evil of his own heart. . . .

Described as ". . . tremendous, an irate, steely black steeple,"[1] the tree is a part of the senior class obstacle course in their preparation for war and is the focal center of the first part of the novel. As the Biblical tree of knowledge it is the means by which Gene will renounce the Eden-like summer peace of Devon and, in so doing, both fall from innocence and at the same time prepare himself for the second world war. As in the fall of Genesis, there is concerning this tree a temptation.

Taunted by Phineas to jump from the tree, Gene says: "I was damned if I'd climb it. The hell with it." (p. 6.) Aside from its obvious school boy appropriateness, his remark foreshadows his later fall. Standing high in the tree after surrendering to Finny's dare, Gene hears Finny, who had characterized his initial jump as his contribution to the war effort, reintroduce the war motif, saying: "When they torpedo the troopship, you can't stand around admiring the view. Jump!" (p. 8.) As Gene hears these words, he wonders: "What was I doing up here anyway? Why did I let Finny talk me into stupid things like this? Was he getting some kind of hold over me?" Then as Gene jumps, he thinks: "With the sensation that I was throwing my life away, I jumped into space." (pp. 8–9.)

What Finny represents in Gene's temptation is the pure spirit of man (mirrored in the boy Finny) answering its need to share the experience of life and innocent love. For Finny the war and the tree, which represents a training ground for the war, are only boyish delights. The reality of war is lost upon him because he is constitutionally pure and incapable of malice. That this is so can be seen from Gene's later statement regarding Finny as a potential soldier. He says:

> They'd get you some place at the front and there'd be a lull in the fighting, and the next thing anyone knew you'd be over with the Germans or the Japs, asking if they'd like to field a baseball team against our side. You'd be sitting in one of their command posts, teaching them English. Yes, you'd get confused and borrow one of their uniforms, and you'd lend them one of yours. Sure, that's just what would happen. You'd get things so scrambled up nobody would know who to fight any more. You'd make a mess, a terrible mess, Finny, out of the war. (p. 173.)

The tragedy of the novel ultimately is that Gene is not capable of maintaining the spiritual purity that distinguishes Phineas and so must as he discovers his own savagery betray Phineas.

Once the two jumps have been effected, a bond has been cemented between the two. But as Gene and Finny walk up to the dormitories, Gene forgets that he has, in following Finny, denied the adult rules which regulate human relationships, and lapses back into his concern for authority. Falling into his "West Point stride," he says: "We'd better hurry or we'll be late for dinner." Phineas, however, objects to Gene's having forgotten what is exemplified in the jumping from the tree and trips Gene. After a brief scuffle the two boys resume their walk. Gene, then, acknowledges that he has succumbed to Finny. He says:

> Then Finny trapped me again in his strongest trap, that is, I suddenly became his collaborator. As we walked rapidly along, I abruptly resented the bell and my West Point stride and hurrying and conforming. Finny was right. (p. 11.)

To acknowledge visibly his giving up the rules of Devon, Gene now trips Finny, and the two are united in a boy's conspiracy to elude adulthood and its rules.

Gene's Envy

The progress of the novel after this joining of Phineas and Gene is the progress of Gene's growing envy of Finny. Incapable of the spiritual purity of Phineas, Gene finds himself jealous of Finny's ability to flout Devon rules in his quest to enjoy an "unregulated friendliness" with the adult world. Gene says apropos of several incidents involving Finny and the Devon rules:

> I was beginning to see that Phineas could get away with anything. I couldn't help envying him that a little, which was perfectly normal. There was no harm in envying even your best friend a little. (p. 17.)

and

> This time he wasn't going to get away with it. I could feel myself becoming unexpectedly excited at that. (p. 19.)

And when Finny does evade punishment, Gene thinks:

> He had gotten away with everything. I felt a sudden stab of disappointment. That was because I just wanted to see some more excitement; that must have been it. (p. 20.)

It is during a bicycle trip to the beach on the morning of the day on which Gene will push Finny from the tree that Finny confides to Gene that he is his best friend. Gene, however, cannot respond. He says: "I nearly did. But something held me back. Perhaps I was stopped by that level of feeling, deeper than thought, which contains the truth." (p. 38.) The effect of this trip is to cause Gene to fail a trigonometry test and thereby to bring his hatred of Finny into the open. Inventing reasons to explain what exists only in his projecting it upon Phineas, Gene says as he realizes what he thinks is Finny's plot:

> Then a second realization broke. . . . Finny had deliberately set out to wreck my studies. . . . That way he, the great athlete, would be way ahead of me. It was all cold trickery, it was all calculated, it was all enmity. (p. 43.)

Later, just before he will shake Finny from the tree, Gene confronts Phineas with his suspicions. Finny's surprise at the charge is such that Gene realizes its falsity. Confronted with the evident truth of Finny's denial, Gene understands his inferiority to Phineas and his own moral ugliness, made the more so when juxtaposed to Finny's innocence. It is this realization that prompts his conscious shaking of the tree, which casts Phineas to the earth and which serves as Gene's initiation into the ignorance and moral blackness of the human heart.

Returning to the fall session without Phineas, Gene finds that peace has deserted Devon. And replacing the freedom of his careless summer are the rules of Devon, to which Gene now gives his allegiance.

Unable to take part in the boyish activities and sports of Devon because of his guilt, Gene attempts to find anonymity in a dead-end job as assistant crew manager. But here, confronted with the arrogance of Cliff Quackenbush (about whom there is an aura of undefined ugliness which separates him from the other boys), Gene is forced to defend Phineas from a slighting remark. This fight between Gene and Quackenbush concludes with their tumbling into the Naguamsett River.

Both the Naguamsett and the Devon flow through the grounds of the school; but it had been into the Devon, a familiar and bucolic river suggestive of Eden, that Finny and Gene had jumped from the tree. But after his fall from innocence, Gene experiences a baptism of a different sort as he plunges into the Naguamsett—a saline, marshy, ugly river "governed by unimaginable factors like the Gulf Stream, the Polar Ice Cap, and the moon."

In what Gene says after his fall into the Naguamsett is introduced the latter parts of the paired symbols that were discussed earlier—the winter, the Naguamsett, and the war (fight). Gene says of his fall:

> I had taken a shower to wash off the sticky salt of the Naguamsett River—going into the Devon was like taking a refreshing shower itself, you never had to clean up after it, but the Naguamsett was something else entirely. I had never been in it before; it seemed appropriate that my baptism there had taken place on the first day of this winter session, and that I had been thrown into it, in the middle of a fight. (p. 73.)

And just as Gene has gone from the innocence exemplified in the Devon River to the experience of the Naguamsett, so the peaceful Devon River itself, whose course "was determined by some familiar hills a little inland" and which "rose among highland farms and forests," ultimately must succumb to the cosmic force of the world; for it, after passing "at the end of its course through the school grounds," then "threw itself with little spectacle over a small waterfall beside the diving dam, and into the turbid Naguamsett." (p. 64.)

Gene's Regeneration

The return of Phineas to Devon signals the rejuvenation and regeneration of Gene. Immediately prior to Finny's return, Gene had discovered in Brinker's announcement of his intention to enlist a chance to close the door on the pain that has haunted him since his crime against Finny. He says of enlistment and its offer to allow him to consecrate himself to the destruction of the war and to his own capacity for evil:

> To enlist. To slam the door impulsively on the past, to shed everything down to my last bit of clothing, to break the pattern of my life—that complex design I had been weaving alone since birth with all its dark threads,

its unexplainable symbols set against a conventional background of domestic white and schoolboy blue, all those tangled strands which required the dexterity of a virtuoso to keep flowing—I yearned to take giant military shears to it, snap! bitten off in an instant, and nothing left in my hands but spools of khaki which could weave only plain, flat, khaki design, however twisted they might be.

Not that it would be a good life. The war would be deadly all right. But I was used to finding something deadly in things that attracted me; there was something deadly lurking in anything I wanted, anything I loved. And if it wasn't there, as for example with Phineas, then I put it there myself.

But in the war, there was no question about it at all; it was there. (p. 87.)

But with Phineas' return and Gene's realization that Phineas needs him to help him maintain his integrity, Gene finds moral purpose and determines to live out his life at Devon with Finny. He says:

Phineas was shocked at the idea of my leaving. In some way he needed me. He needed me. I was the least trustworthy person he had ever met. I knew that; he knew or should know that too. I had even told him. I had told him. But there was no mistaking the shield of remoteness in his face and voice. He wanted me around. The war then passed away from me, and dreams of enlistment and escape and a clean start lost their meaning for me. (pp. 93–94.)

With Gene's resolution, peace returns to Devon and the war is forgotten. . . .

The Phineas-inspired Devon Winter Carnival is the occasion during which Gene is to be paraded in all his Olympic glory, signifying that he, through consecrating himself to Finny's tutelage, has become like Phineas. About this winter carnival and his brilliant decathlon performance, Gene says:

It wasn't the cider which made me surpass myself, it was this liberation we had torn from the gray encroachments of 1943, the escape we had concocted, this afternoon of momentary, illusory, special and separate peace. (p. 121.)

Yet even as this illusion is achieved, a telegram arrives from Leper, an "escapee" from the war, come back to destroy Gene's illusion of withdrawing from the war. . . .

Gene's Understanding

The reconciliation of Gene and Finny after Finny's refusal to accept Brinker's "f___ing facts" and his fall provides the culmination of the novel. Questioned by Finny, Gene denies that his pushing of Phineas was personal. Beginning to understand himself, Gene says: "It was just some ignorance inside me, some crazy thing inside me, something blind, that's all." (p. 174.) And joined with this realization is Gene's admission that war, despite Phineas, does exist and that it grows out of the ignorance of the human heart. In rejecting Brinker's thesis that wars can be laid to one's parents and their generation, Gene says: ". . . It seemed clear that wars were not made by generations and their special stupidities, but that wars were made instead by something ignorant in the human heart." (p. 183.) Gene has discovered that his private evil, which caused him to hurt Phineas, is the same evil—only magnified—that results in war.

Finny alone, Gene now knows, was incapable of malice. Reviewing his relation with Phineas, Gene tells of Finny's way "of sizing up the world with erratic and entirely personal reservations, letting its rocklike facts sift through and be accepted only a little at a time, only as much as he could assimilate without a sense of chaos and loss." (p. 184.)

Because of his ability to admit only as much of the ugliness of life as he could assimilate, Phineas was unique. Gene says:

No one else I have ever met could do this. All others at some point found something in themselves pitted violently against something in the world around them.

With those of my year this point often came when they grasped the fact of the war. When they began to feel that there was this overwhelmingly hostile thing in the world with them, then the simplicity and unity of their characters broke and they were not the same again.

Phineas alone had escaped this. He possessed an extra vigor, a heightened confidence in himself, a serene capacity for affection which saved him. Nothing as he was growing up at home, nothing at Devon, nothing even about the war had broken his harmonious and natural unity. So at last I had. (p. 184.)

It is because of his having known and loved Phineas that Gene can recognize that hatred springs from a greater evil that is within. It is the realization of this that releases him from the hysteria of the war, which now moves from its controlling position off-stage onto the campus of Devon in the form of the parachute riggers.

Unlike his friends who had sought through some building of defenses to ward off the inevitability of evil, Gene has come to see that this enemy never comes from without, but always from within. He knows, moreover, that there is no defense to be built, only an acceptance and purification of oneself through love. Such a love did he share with Phineas in a private gypsy summer. And it is because of the purity of this love that he is able to survive his fall from innocence.

Note

1. John Knowles, *A Separate Peace* (New York: Macmillan, 1960), p. 6. Subsequent references to this novel will be to this edition and will be incorporated into the text.

RONALD WEBER ON NARRATIVE METHOD IN THE NOVEL

Holden's relation to the experience of the novel illustrates a major problem of first-person telling. Although the method, by narrowing the sense of distance separating reader, narrator, and fictional experience, gains a quality of immediacy and freshness, it tends for the same reason to prohibit insight or understanding. This latter point has been clearly noted by Brooks and Warren:

> First-person narration tends to shorten the distance between the reader and the fictional character; for instance, the character narrating his own story tends to give us the world strictly in his own terms, in his own feelings and attitudes, and he can scarcely see himself in a large context. He tends to reveal himself rather than to pass judgment upon himself, to give comments about himself, or to analyze himself. Such judgments, comments, and analyses exist in such a story, but they exist by implication, and the reader must formulate them for himself.

Understanding exists in *Catcher*, but not self-understanding for Holden. Because of the intense method of narration, narrowing rather than enlarging the sense of distance in the novel, understanding exists only for the reader, and then only by implication. This situation, as we shall see, is wholly congenial to Salinger's thematic intention; Knowles, however, seeks a different end, and therefore he must somehow modify the effect of his narrative method.

Unlike Holden, Gene Forrester is separated by a broad passage of time from the experience he relates. "I went back to the Devon School not long ago," Gene says in the novel's opening sentence, "and found it looking oddly newer than when I was a student there fifteen years before." That this lapse in time between the experience and the telling has brought understanding is also established early. "Looking back now across fifteen years," Gene says a few paragraphs later, "I could see with great clarity the fear I had lived in. . . ." Although Knowles quickly leaves the distant perspective and turns to immediate scene, he keeps the reader aware that Gene is looking back on the experience with a mature vision. At one point, for example, the distant perspective suddenly opens up at the end of a scene when Gene says: "But in a week I had forgotten that, and I have never since forgotten the dazed look on Finny's face when he thought that on the first day of his return to Devon I was going to desert him." Later, beginning a chapter, Knowles reestablishes the perspective with a long passage that again looks ahead of the present action:

> That night I made for the first time the kind of journey which later became the monotonous routine of my life: traveling through an unknown countryside from one unknown settlement to another. The next year this became the dominant activity, or rather passivity, of my army career, not fighting, not marching, but this kind of nighttime ricochet; for as it turned out I never got to the war.

The distant point of the narration allows a detachment that permits Gene the mastery of his experience. Even when Knowles gives over the narrative wholly to immediate scene the reader is reminded, sometimes with a phrase, at other times with an entire passage, of the perspective. The war, in addition, serves to create an increased sense of distance, a removal in attitude, within the story. Although the war touches Devon School only slightly—one of the joys of the summer session is that it seems totally removed from the world of war—it cannot be forgotten or ignored for long; it exists not only as an event that stands between the experience of the novel and Gene's telling, but as an event that, at the very moment of the experience, dominates the life of each character. "The war," Gene says in retrospect, "was and is reality for me. I still instinctively live and think in its atmosphere." The anticipation of war forces Gene and his companions into a slight yet significant detachment from their life at Devon—a life that, at times, seems unimportant and even unreal—and towards an unusual amount of serious, if carefully guarded, reflection. The relation between the fact of war and the atmosphere of detachment or removal in the novel—removal, again, necessary for understanding—can be seen in Phineas' disclosure that, despite his humorous disavowal of the existence of the war, he has been trying for some time to enlist:

> I'll *hate* it *everywhere* if I'm not in this war [he tells Gene]! Why do you think I kept saying there wasn't any war all winter? I was going to keep on saying it until two seconds after I got a letter from Ottawa or Chungking or some place saying, "Yes, you can enlist with us. . . ." Then there would have been a war.

Similarly, the war serves to remove Gene from his immediate experience and to provoke serious self-scrutiny:

> To enlist [he thinks in response to a day spent freeing snowbound trains in a railroad yard as part of the war effort]. To slam the door impulsively on the past, to shed everything down to my last bit of clothing, to break the pattern of my life—that complex design I had been weaving since birth with all its dark threads, its unexplainable symbols set against a conventional background of domestic white and schoolboy blue, all those tangled strands which required the dexterity of a virtuoso to keep flowing—I yearned to take giant military shears to it, snap! bitten off in an instant, and nothing left in my hands but spools of khaki which could weave only a plain, flat, khaki design, however twisted they might be.

The depth of insight revealed in the passage is made possible both by the narrator's removal in time from the experience and by the existence within the experience of the war as a focus of attention outside of him. Finally, the passage suggests how the central dramatic event of the story, Gene's involvement in the injury of Phineas, adds to the atmosphere of detachment in the novel. The injury, which occurs early in the story and underlies the bulk of the narrative, is another force thrusting Gene away from his immediate experience and towards self-scrutiny; as such, it combines with the distant point of the narration and the existence of war to create the broad quality of detachment that makes understanding both possible and plausible.

Gene comes to self-understanding only gradually through a series of dramatic episodes, as we shall see; the final extent of his understanding can, however, be indicated by a passage from the concluding chapter. "I was ready for the war," he says, thinking ahead to his entry into the army, "now that I no longer had any hatred to contribute to it. My fury was gone, I felt it gone, dried up at the course, withered and lifeless." This final awareness contrasts sharply with Holden Caulfield's lack of self-understanding at the end of *Catcher*. While Holden, looking back on his experience, thinks he may be somewhat changed, Gene is certain he is a radically different person. This differing response of the characters to the experience they relate is additionally underscored for the reader by the tone of their narration. In each case, Holden and Gene, indicate their relation to their experience as much by how they speak as by what they say and when they say it. Holden's voice, uncertain at times and dogmatic at others, is always exuberant and emotional; it is a voice vividly responsive to the experience of the novel but one that suggests little mastery of it. Gene's voice, on the other hand, is dispassionate, reflective, and controlled; it is, in his own words, a voice from which fury is gone, dried up at its source long before the telling begins. If Holden's voice is that of the restless adolescent groping for an uncertain maturity, Gene's is a voice looking back on adolescence after the hard passage to maturity has been won.

It is clear that Knowles, to return to Professor Halio's phrase, does not fall into the "smart-wise idiom made fashionable" by Salinger's novel. He does not follow in Salinger's wake because of the important variation he works on the method of first-person narration used in *Catcher*. By attempting to maintain a sense of distance within a narrative method that naturally tends to narrow distance, he sacrifices some of the method's freshness to gain depth and insight. In *Catcher* the reader, with Holden, tends to respond to the experience with feeling rather than knowledge; understanding exists for him in the novel only by implication. In *A Separate Peace* the reader, with Gene, remains partially detached from the experience, able to examine and reflect upon it; and understanding can finally take the form of direct statement.

At this point we can begin to see some connection between Knowles's narrative method and his thematic concern. Again, comparison with *Catcher* is useful. Both novels, in a broad and very basic sense, are concerned with the response of the central character to an awareness of evil in the world; they are narratives in which the characters confront, during a concentrated period, part of the reality of life. In face of this reality Holden Caulfield suffers a severe physical and mental breakdown. At the end of the novel, when Holden admits he misses the people he has told about—the assorted phonies who represent the world—the reader is to understand that he now has begun to make some beginning accommodation with that world. Holden of course does not understand this change; it is, as we have said, merely a new feeling, a feeling of missing people he previously despised. Although it is clear that some change has taken place in Holden, it is important to see that it is explained in terms of other people; what must in fact be an inner change—Holden arriving at some peace within himself—is communicated in exterior terms.

In the course of his maturing process, Gene Forrester likewise must confront the fact of evil in the world. But in this case the location of that evil is quite different. At the very beginning of the novel, in a passage quoted earlier, Gene, looking back fifteen years, says he can see with great clarity the "fear" he had lived in at Devon School and that he has succeeded in making his "escape" from. Even now, he adds, he can feel "fear's echo," and this in turn leads him back to the direct experience of the story. The meaning of this experience is to be found in the development of the words *fear* and *escape*—in Gene's growing realization of what they mean as well as what they do not mean.

When his friend and roommate Phineas breaks a Devon swimming record and then refuses to let anyone know about it, Gene is deeply troubled:

Was he trying to impress me or something? Not tell anybody? When he had broken a school record without a day of practice? I knew he was serious about it, so I didn't tell anybody. Perhaps for that reason his accomplishment took root in my mind and grew rapidly in the darkness where I was forced to hide it.

Later, during an overnight escapade on an oceanside beach, Phineas causes him another moment of uncertainty. Just before the two boys fall asleep, Phineas frankly declares that Gene is his "best pal."

> It was a courageous thing to say [Gene reflects]. Exposing a sincere emotion nakedly like that at the Devon School was the next thing to suicide. I should have told him then that he was my best friend also and rounded off what he had said. I started to; I nearly did. But something held me back. Perhaps I was stopped by that level of feeling, deeper than thought, which contains the truth.

Gene's troubled feelings rise to the level of thought in a following scene during which he comes to the conclusion that Phineas, the school's finest athlete, envies him his academic success. This knowledge instantly shatters any notions he has had of "affection and partnership and sticking by someone and relying on someone absolutely in the jungle of a boys' school." He now sees that Phineas is his rival, not his friend, and this in turn explains his failure to respond properly when Phineas broke the swimming record and when he confessed his friendship. He now sees that he has been envious of Phineas too—envious to the point of complete enmity. Out of the wreck of their friendship this dual rivalry emerges as a saving bit of knowledge:

> I found it [Gene says]. I found a single sustaining thought. The thought was, You and Phineas are even already. You are even in enmity. You are both coldly driving ahead for yourselves alone. You did hate him for breaking

that school swimming record, but so what? He hated you for getting an A in every course but one last term.

Their mutual hatred not only explains Gene's inability to respond properly to Phineas, but it relieves him of any further anxiety:

> I felt better. Yes, I sensed it like the sweat of relief when nausea passes away; I felt better. We were even after all, even in enmity. The deadly rivalry was on both sides after all.

Gene's sense of relief, it turns out, is of short duration. When Phineas, in a moment of seriousness, urges him to stick with his studies rather than come along on a campus diversion, Gene suddenly sees he has been wrong—Phineas has never envied him. During a scene immediately following, in which he and Phineas perch in a tree waiting to leap into a river below, Gene is overwhelmed by the implications of this new insight:

> Any fear I had ever had of the tree was nothing beside this. It wasn't my neck, but my understanding which was menaced. He had never been jealous of me for a second. Now I knew that there never was and never could have been any rivalry between us. I was not of the same quality as he. I couldn't stand this.

It is at this moment that he causes Phineas to fall from the tree, an "accident" that cripples him and ends his athletic career. After watching Phineas crash through the branches of the tree and hit the bank, Gene jumps confidently into the river, "every trace of my fear of this forgotten."

It is Phineas' innocence that Gene cannot endure. As long as he can believe Phineas shares his enmity, he can find relief; but with this assurance gone, he stands condemned before himself and must strike out against his tormentor. *Fear*, again, is the key word. Fear in this instance is the emotional response to the discovery of hate, the vast depths of enmity that exist within the human heart. Gene loses his fear and achieves his separate, personal peace only when he acknowledges this fundamental truth. It is a truth that he must first recognize and then accept; he can neither avoid it, as he tries to do in his first encounter with Phineas after the accident, nor flee from it, as he again seeks to do when Leper charges that he always has been a "savage underneath." He can find escape from fear only in the acceptance of its true source and the location of that source. Gene must come to see and endure the truth, as he finally does in a climactic scene just before Phineas dies from a second fall, that his fear is the product not of rivalry nor of circumstance but of "some ignorance inside me, some crazy thing inside me, something blind."

None of Gene's companions at Devon could bring themselves to face this inner source of their fear. When they began to feel this "overwhelmingly hostile thing in the world with them," they looked beyond themselves and felt themselves violently pitted against something in the outer world. When they experienced this "fearful shock" of the "sighting of the enemy," they began an "obsessive labor of defense" and began to parry the menace they thought they saw facing them. They all

> constructed at infinite cost to themselves these Maginot Lines against this enemy they thought they saw across the frontier, this enemy who never attacked that way—if he ever attacked at all; if he was indeed the enemy.

The infinite cost in this case is the loss of self-knowledge. Only Phineas is an exception; only Phineas "never was afraid" because only he "never hated anyone." Phineas alone is free of the awareness of that hostile thing that is to be found not across any battlefield but within the fortress itself. As the archetypal innocent, he must serve as the sacrifice to Gene's maturity. "I was ready for the war," Gene says at the end, "now that I no longer had any hatred to contribute to it. My fury was gone. . . . Phineas had absorbed it and taken it with him, and I was rid of it forever."

Gene Forrester comes to learn that his war, the essential war, is fought out on the battlefield within. Peace comes only when he faces up to this fact. The only escape, the price of peace, is self-awareness. One finds the resolution of Holden Caulfield's war, on the other hand, beyond him, in his relation to society. As Holden flees a corrupt world he is driven increasingly in upon himself, but towards collapse rather than awareness. Salinger presents the hope that is finally raised for him not in terms of self-knowledge but in the ability to move out of himself. It is not, then, awareness that is offered for him so much as a kind of accommodation; he must somehow learn to live, as Mr. Antolini tells him, with what is sickening and corrupt in human behavior. Although this implies facing up to what is corrupt in his own nature, this is not Salinger's emphasis. He seeks to focus the novel outside Holden rather than within him; and for this the conventional method of first-person narration with its tendency to narrow and intensify the story, eliminating the sense of distance vital for the narrator's self-understanding, is admirably suited. Knowles, using a similar but skillfully altered narrative method, develops a very different theme—that awareness, to put it baldly, must precede accommodation, that to look without before having first searched within is tragically to confuse the human condition. To convey his theme Knowles modifies the first-person narrative to create for both narrator and reader an atmosphere of detachment that permits the novel to be focused within Gene, where, he shows, a basic truth of life is to be found.

While the reader may come to feel the experience of *A Separate Peace* somewhat less than that of *Catcher*, he eventually knows it more. While Salinger may give him a stronger sense of life, Knowles provides a clearer statement about life. Although the two novels work towards different ends with different means, they help finally to illustrate, in their separate ways, the close functional relation of meaning and method of telling in carefully-wrought fiction.

PETER WOLFE ON THE IMPACT OF THE NOVEL

A Separate Peace shapes the problem of man's inherent savagery to American culture. In contrast to the characters of D. H.

Lawrence, those of Knowles do not discharge their deepest impulses sexually. Instead they retrace the familiar American fictional pattern of immersing themselves in the past. But where Fitzgerald's Gatsby hankers after the glamor of first love and Miller's Willy Loman looks back to the days when salesmanship was adventurous, Knowles's Gene Forrester reaches back much further. He sounds the uncharted seas of our common humanity and in so doing both undoes the work of civilization and reawakens the wild meaninglessness of primitive man. . . .

The first chapter of *A Separate Peace* shows Gene Forrester returning to Devon fifteen years after the key incident of his life—that of shaking his best friend Phineas out of a tree and shattering his leg. Mingling memory and fear, Gene is not only the archetypal criminal who returns to the scene of his crime or the American fictional hero who retreats into a private past. His return to Devon is purposive, even compulsive. His neglecting to mention his job, his family, or his home suggests that he has none of these things, even though he is past the age of thirty. He relives his act of treachery and the events surrounding it in the hope of recovering the separate peace of the summer of 1942.

Gene interests us chiefly because of his moral ambiguity: whereas he accepts his malevolence, he also resists indulging it at the expense of others. Fear of unleashing his inherent wickedness explains his inertia since Devon's 1942–43 academic year. It also explains his psychological bloc. His first-person narration is laced with self-abuse, special pleading, flawed logic, and evasiveness. As has been suggested, self-exploration is dangerous work, and Gene cannot be blamed if he sometimes cracks under the strain. Out of joint with both himself and his time, he subjects to reason an area of being which is neither rational nor reducible to rational formulas. Although the sum will not add, he has no choice but to try to add the sum if he wants to re-enter the human community.

Like the novel's memoir technique, Gene Forrester's name certifies that *A Separate Peace* is his book. Of the forest, Gene is a primitive, bloodthirsty woodlander; his occasional self-disclosures spell out the urgency of his death-pull: "I was used to finding something deadly in things that attracted me; there was always something deadly lurking in anything I wanted, anything I loved. And if it wasn't there . . . I put it there myself." (87)

The forest has negative associations throughout the book. At one point Gene is accused of undermining his health by "smoking like a forest fire." (112) Elsewhere the forest is equated with the raw icy wilderness stretching from the northern edge of Devon School to "the far unorganized tips of Canada." (22) As it is in Emily Dickinson, summer for Knowles is the time of flowing beauty and intensity of being. The Sommers family are the most vital characters in *Indian Summer*, and the gipsy spree of Gene and Phineas takes place during summer term.

Devon represents the last outpost of civilization to Gene. It wards off the primitive madness encroaching from the great northern forests, and it shields its students from the organized madness of World War II. Devon's 1942 summer term, the first in its history, is giving Gene and Phineas their last reprieve from a war-racked world. At sixteen, the boys and their classmates are the oldest students at Devon excused from taking both military subjects and preinduction physical exams.

In contrast to this freedom, winter brings loss, unreason, and hardness of heart. Nor is the heartless irrationality equated with Gene's forest background uncommon. His first name universalizes his glacial cruelty. While Phineas is a sport (who happens to excel in sports), Gene is generic, his barbarism deriving from his North American forebears. And the fact that he is a southerner shows how deeply this northern madness has bitten into American life.

The first object of Gene's return visit to Devon is the tree he ousted Phineas from fifteen years before. James Ellis places the tree in a Christian context by calling it "the Biblical tree of knowledge."[5] His interpretation is amply justified by parallels between the novel and orthodox Christianity: everything in the boys' lives changes for the worst after the tree incident, the tree and Christ's crucifix are both wood, the slab of light under the door that announces Phineas's return to Devon is yellow, the color of Judas and betrayal, and Gene chins himself thirty times the next day in the school's gymnasium.

Yet Christian myth fails to exhaust the tree's meaning. Its rootedness in the earth, its riverbank location, and its overarching branches suggest organic life. Lacking a single meaning, the tree stands for reality itself. Knowles develops this powerful inclusiveness by projecting the tree to several levels of being. For the tree not only exists forcibly at more than one dimension; it also brings together different aspects of reality. Over the spectrum of Gene's life, it is by turns an occasion for danger, friendship, betrayal and regret. Remembered as "a huge lone spike dominating the riverbank, forbidding as an artillery piece," the tree is so much "smaller" and "shrunken by age" (5) fifteen years later that Gene has trouble recognizing it.

Nonetheless, as something more than a physical datum, it marks the turning point of Gene's life and colors the rest of his narrative. The furniture in the home of one of his teachers "shot out menacing twigs," (17) and the tree combines metaphorically with both the War and the aboriginal northern frost to create a strong impression of lostness. The tree's combining power, in fact, is as great as its power to halt or cut short. For while it marks the end of the gipsy summer of 1942, it also yokes Gene's past and present lives.

The victim of the tree incident, Phineas, is best summarized by a phrase Knowles uses in *Double Vision* to describe modern Greeks—"a full life lived naturally."[6] Nor is the classical parallel askew. Phineas's name resembles phonetically that of Phidias, who helped set the standard of all-around excellence that marked the golden age of Pericles. (The nickname, "Finny," suggests in another key a throwback to a morality earlier than our Christian-western ethical system.) Although "an extraordinary athlete . . . the best athlete in the school," (7) Finny stands under five feet nine and weighs only a hundred and fifty pounds. His athletic prowess stems not from brawn but from his superb co-ordination and vitality.

Interestingly, the trophies he wins are for gentlemanly conduct. Finny's mastery goes beyond sports. His great gift is the ability to respond clearly and fully: his "unthinking unity of movement" (9) and his favorite expressions, "naturally" and "perfectly okay," express the harmony and interrelatedness of his life. Finny can afford casualness because he gives himself wholly to his undertakings. There is no room for self-consciousness in this dynamic life-mode. There is no room either for formalized rules. Finny's commitment to life overrides the requirements of reason and law, but not out of innate lawlessness. His responses strike so deeply that, while they sometimes make nonsense of conventional morality, they create their own scale of values.

Finny's organicism also sets the style and tempo of the free, unclassifiable summer of 1942. It must be noted that the separate peace Finny and Gene carve out is no idyllic escape from reality. By founding the Super Suicide Society of the Summer Session, membership in which requires a dangerous leap into the Devon River, the boys admit both danger and death into their golden gipsy days. Accordingly, the game of Blitzball, which Finny invents the same summer, includes the bellicosity and treachery that perhaps count as humanity's worst features: "Since we're all enemies, we can and will turn on each other all the time." (29) Nevertheless, the boys rejoice in Blitzball and, while they sustain a fierce level of competition, they manage to avoid injuries.

For opponents do not inflict pain in the world of *A Separate Peace*; the worst menaces dwell not in rivalry but in friendship. Gene and Phineas become best friends, but Gene cannot live with Finny's goodness. Finny's helping Gene overcome fear and his opening his friend to bracing new adventures rouses Gene's worst traits. Man is a hating rather than a loving animal. Franziska Lynne Greiling summarizes deftly the stages leading to Gene's savaging of Finny:

> At the beginning, Gene thought of himself as Phineas' equal, first in excellence, then in enmity. Discovering Phineas incapable of hatred, Gene has to face his own moral ugliness and then strikes down Phineas for inadvertently revealing it to him.[7]

The summary bears close scrutiny. What finally unlooses Gene's venom is Finny's magnanimity. Although Gene's treachery in Chapter Four strikes explosively, incidents in earlier chapters justify it dramatically. Finny's saving Gene at the end of Chapter Two when he nearly falls out of the tree during a mission of the Super Suicide Society compounds his felony. Gene turns the act of loyalty and sacrifice into an occasion for resentment. Instead of being grateful to Finny for saving his life, he blames his friend for tempting him to jump from the tree in the first place.

Chapter Three puts Finny beyond such commonplace resentment. Here he breaks the school's swimming record for the hundred-yard free style but insists that his feat be kept a secret. Chapter Four shows Gene incontestably that Finny has both outclassed and outmanned him. Whereas Gene bases all his human ties on rivalry, he must bolt down the knowledge that Finny is free of envy. This generosity upsets Gene's entire life-mode: "Now I knew that there never was and never could have been any rivalry between us. I was not of the same quality as he." (49) . . .

By shaking his friend out of the tree, Gene obeys an urge deeper than reason or wounded vanity. But his act of aboriginal madness is empty. The things that happen to him after his treachery demonstrates the pointless waste of violence.

But they do not draw the sting of his violent tendencies. Gene's first reaction to Finny's shattered leg is complex. Since Finny's vitality diminishes Gene, he is glad to be rid of his friend. Finny's confinement in the Infirmary lets Gene become Finny. He calls Finny "noble" (50) and in the next paragraph, after putting on his friend's clothes, says that he feels "like some nobleman." (51) Even the relaxed, supple style in which he writes his memoir fits with his desire to merge with his male ideal.

Ironically, Finny is just as eager as Gene to switch identities. Rather than accusing him of treachery or languishing in self-pity, he tries to recover some of his lost splendor through his friend. Knowles says at one point in the book that a broken bone, once healed, is strongest in the place where the break occurred. The statement applies to Finny's recuperative powers. His athletic career ended, Finny acquires new skills and learns to exist on a new plane while preserving his high standard of personal loyalty.

Everything and nothing have changed. Buoyed up by his heroic ethic, he returns to Devon midway through the winter term and begins training Gene for the 1944 Olympic Games. His training a groundling athlete for a match that will never be held points up the strength of his moral vision. Finny denies the reality of World War II because he knows instinctively that man can only fulfill himself when the ordinary civilized processes of life are reasonably secure.

The two boys institute a routine based on their best gifts: while Finny coaches Gene on the cinderpath and in the gym, Gene helps Finny with his studies. The routine is kinetic. Finny's organizing of the Devon Winter Carnival, like the Blitzball and the Super Suicide Society of the previous summer, represents an acceptance of reality. But the Carnival reflects an even braver commitment to imperfection than the summer romps. It takes no special gifts to make merry in the summer. By celebrating winter, though, Phineas opts for life's harshness as well as its joys; and by choosing the northern reaches of the school as a site for the carnival, he certifies fun and friendship alongside the icy savagery clawing down from the unpeopled North.

Gene ends this regimen because he cannot forgive Phineas for submitting to his brutality. He determines to make his cruelty a counterforce to Phineas's loyalty and courage. After Phineas breaks his leg falling on the slick marble steps of the First Academy Building, Gene follows him to the Infirmary. But instead of showing compassion for his stricken friend, his thoughts turn inward. Astonishingly, his attitude is one of cool self-acceptance. "I couldn't escape a confusing sense of living through all of this before—Phineas in the Infirmary, and myself responsible. I seemed to be less shocked by it now than I had been the first time last August." (170)

Gene's detachment imparts the final horror to his actions. Yet Phineas can take his worst thrusts. Although he can no longer control his muscular reactions, his mind stays whole. His body breaks before his spirit; he accepts Gene's treachery, and when he dies he has transcended it. Nobody in the book can come near enough to him to kill him. He dies as he had lived— untouched by human baseness. While his broken leg is being set, some of the bone-marrow escapes into his bloodstream and lodges in his heart. In that bone-marrow produces the body's life-giving red corpuscles, Phineas dies from an overplus and a richness of animal vigor.

Gene's barbarism finds another outlet in Elwin "Leper" Lepellier. Although Leper is not so well perceived as Finny, he serves structurally as Finny's foil. Whereas Finny attracts people, Leper is an outsider; and Leper matches Finny's physical breakdown by cracking psychologically. A solitary at school, he is crushed by the tighter discipline and organization practiced by the Army. But the organized madness of the Army, while wrecking his sanity, sharpens his insight. He tells Gene, "You always were a savage underneath," (128) and later in the book he describes the tree episode with a poetic accuracy that lays bare the core of Gene's treachery.

Yet none of Leper's hearers can understand him. Finny, on the other hand, communicates by bodily movements and is always perfectly understood. Leper's oppositeness to Finny reveals two important things about Gene's savagery: its all-inclusive sweep and its static nature. Although Finny and Leper both grow, Gene is hunkered in his wickedness. In the same way that primitive societies are the least free, he can neither explain nor change himself once he gives in to his primitive drives. Not only does he rake his two best friends; he justifies his butchery: "a mind was clouded and a leg was broken— maybe these should be thought of as minor and inevitable mishaps in the accelerating rush. The air around us was filled with much worse things." (170)

The Leper–Finny doubling motif is but one example of Knowles's fondness for sharp contrast as a structural principle. The author also plays the carefree summer of 1942 against the winter term that follows. He manages his contrast by means of the various associations created by the intervening season, fall. . . .

The daily character of life at Devon also expresses the darkening shift from summer to winter. The change in mood is observable the first day of winter term: "We had been an idiosyncratic, leaderless band in the summer . . . Now the official class leaders and politicians could be seen taking charge." (62) Gene's murder of the "simple, unregulated friendliness" (14) marking the summer term validates the need for restricting man's freedom. Like that of Hawthorne, Knowles's attitude toward the law is complex. If civilization is to survive, then man's intrinsic savagery must be bridled. Yet any formal legal system will prove unreliable. The members of the older generation described in the book cannot claim any natural or acquired superiority over their sons. They stand to blame for the War and also for the congressional investigating committees the novel attacks indirectly.

Rules and restrictions turn out to be just as poor a standard of civilized conduct as feelings. Knowles introduces the character of Brinker Hadley—a classmate of Finny, Leper, and Gene—to point up the murderous cruelty of the law. Significantly, Brinker does not enter the book until the 1942–43 winter term. He makes the distressing point that man tends to use the law not as a check to man's aggressiveness, but as an outlet. Legalistic, rule-bound, and calculating, Brinker only invokes the law in order to frustrate or to punish. Knowles mentions "his Winter Session efficiency" (74) and later calls him "Brinker the Lawgiver" (115) and "Justice incarnate." (151)

But he also reminds us that although justice balances the scales of human conduct, she is also blindfolded. Brinker's blind spot is the life of feeling, his fact-ridden life having ruled out compassion. Brinker, who has a large posterior, or butt, presides from the Butt Room, a cellar which is both the dreariest and the lowest site on the Devon campus. Because Gene could not rise to the example set by Phineas, he must pass muster with Brinker's Butt-Room morality. The tree incident not only drives the boys indoors but also downward—both physically and morally:

The Butt Room was something like a dungeon. . . . On the playing fields we looked like innocent extroverts; and in the Butt Room we looked, very strongly, like criminals. The school's policy, in order to discourage smoking, was to make these rooms as depressing as possible. (75)

The structure of *A Separate Peace* includes the same tensions, stresses, and balances. Chapter Seven, the middle chapter of the novel, is dominated by snow, a common symbol for death. Suitably, the big snowfall of Chapter Seven, like the tree incident of Chapter Four, occurs out of season. Chapter Seven also introduces Brinker Hadley and restores Phineas to Devon. As the chapter advances, the thickening snows envelop Gene; by the end of the chapter, they obstruct all of life. . . .

The technique of the last chapter tallies well with both the events and the morality it describes. Knowles violates the unity of time by leaping ahead several months to June 1943; he also breaks a basic rule of fictional art by introducing an important character in his last chapter. These discordancies are intentional: a novel about disjointedness should have its components out of joint with each other. Accordingly, *A Separate Peace* extends a chapter after Phineas's death and funeral.

But instead of joining its dramatic and thematic climaxes, the last chapter has a scattering effect. Gene's class at Devon has just been graduated, and the boys are shipping out to various branches of the military. The new character, Brinker Hadley's father, is a World War I veteran whose lofty code of patriotism and service means little to the younger generation.

Mr. Hadley cannot, however, be dismissed as a stale anachronism. His argument implies that he knows something the boys have not yet learned. Combat duty is important to him, not as an immediate goal but as a topic to reminisce about in future years. Could Mr. Hadley be suggesting that maturity contains few pleasures and that only a heroic youth can make up for this emptiness? That the boys overlook this implication means little. The chapter is full of communication failures, including the generation rift Mr. Hadley introduces by visiting Devon.

Another new presence at Devon is the U. S. Army. Devon has donated part of its grounds to a Parachute Riggers' school. Appropriately, the sector of the campus used by the soldiers is the Northern Common. But Knowles pulls a stunning reversal by overturning this fine narrative stroke. For although the Army as the collective embodiment of man's aggressiveness invades Devon from the icy North, man's aggressiveness has already established a stronghold at Devon. Likewise, the convoy of jeeps driving through campus stirs no warlike fervor. The boyish troops are "not very bellicose-looking," (178) and the jeeps do not contain weapons but sewing machines.

The logic of the novel makes eminent sense of this unlikely freight: the sewing machines, which will service parachutes, allude to the novel's central metaphor of falling, and the young soldiers will lunge headlong into violence in the same way as Devon's Class of 1943. By the end of the book, the malevolence uncoiling from man's fallen nature has engulfed all.

Except, strangely, for Gene. His savagery already spent, he has no aggressiveness left for the Navy. Although his country is at war, he is at peace. Yet the armistice is false. A man so askew with his environment enjoys no peace. Gene's lack of purpose not only divides him from his country; it separates him from himself. Divided and subdivided, he is fighting a war just as dangerous as his country's. He has not killed his enemy, as he insists. (186)

His return to Devon in his early thirties and his memoir of Devon's 1942–43 academic year prove that his private struggle has outlasted the public holocaust of World War II. Just as the anvil can break the hammer, the tree incident hurts Gene more than it does Finny. The novel turns on the irony that the separate peace mentioned in its title excludes its most vivid presence—its narrator. Gene's fall 1957 visit to Devon fixes the limits of his fallen life. His self-inventory is either a preparation for life or a statement of withdrawal. But the question of whether he can convert his apartness into a new start goes beyond the boundaries of the novel.

Notes
  5. Ellis, p. 313.
  6. Knowles, *Double Vision*, p. 200.
  7. Greiling, p. 1271.

MARVIN E. MENGELING ON MEANING AND MYTH

For John Knowles the mythic journey of *A Separate Peace* involves a paradoxical quest for the ideals of the Golden Age of Greece; paradoxical in that a step backward chronologically in a search for value becomes for man a step forward emotionally.

We are informed from numerous sources that the character of the so-called "golden" Greek consisted of energy and experimentation, but never unaccompanied by the tempering agents of clear judgment and good reason. They were a people of deep curiosity concerning the natural world in which they lived. Study of nature led almost inevitably to an appreciation of its balance and essential simplicity. The Greek concept of the ideal life, then, was grounded in achieving harmony between one's abilities and interests. One should strive for that healthy and happy equilibrium which exists between action and thought. All attempts would prove impotent, however, if individual man did not avoid the dreaded *hubris*, that insolence and pride which separates man from his fellows and sets him at war with harmony. Truly, "man is the measure of all things," but only, to paraphrase Socrates, if man truly knows himself. Harmony and balance, far removed from the haunts of pride and insolence, are a portion of that humanism which Phineas offers Gene.

Phineas, of course, depicts more than just a generalized approach to life, for in a deeper, more exact sense he portrays a god, called by some the most Greek of all the gods, Phoebus Apollo. Phoebus Apollo, god of light and youth—represented in art as handsome, young, athletic—was a beautiful, glowing figure. He was not only the master musician but also the Archer god. Most significantly, Phoebus Apollo was the healer, the god who first taught man the healing art, a specialist in purifications who taught correct procedures for avoiding evils, ills, superstitions, and fears. He was the god of light; in him there was no darkness, no falsehood, but only truth. Due to such brilliant attributes Phoebus Apollo was quite probably confused by the later Greeks with Helios, Greek god of the sun, and for this reason is also known as the sun god, shown in much later art with rays of light shooting from his head. This point is of no small importance when one recalls the many scenes in *A Separate Peace* in which Phineas is directly connected to the sun, and especially those scenes in which rays of sunlight seem to burst from the form of Phineas in silhouette.

It was through the healthy creation of such deities as Phoebus Apollo that the Greek people somehow largely dismissed from their lives the most brutalizing of all human emotions—fear. A world which had been haunted for untold ages by dark and unknown terrors was somehow miraculously changed, in Greece at least, to a world with much beauty, reason, and common sense. It is from the black labyrinth of such a brutalizing emotion as fear that Phineas at last salvages Gene and starts him down the path to a humanistic loyalty, "beginning with him and me and radiating outward past the limits of humanity toward spirits and clouds and stars" (p. 33).

There is an obvious pattern of Greek allusions in *A Separate Peace*. At one important point Phineas is described as "Greek inspired and Olympian" (p. 136). He is athletic and beautiful, blazing with "sunburned health" (p. 13). He walks before Gene in a "continuous flowing balance" (p. 97) that acknowledges an "unemphatic unity of strength" (p. 7). Though Gene, as any boy his age, is often given to imaginative hyperbole (as we all are when our Gods are involved), there is no doubt that to him and the other boys Phineas is "unique" (p. 47). Behind his "controlled ease" (p. 33) there rests the "strength of five people" (p. 91). And even if he cannot carry a tune as well as he carries other people, Phineas loves all music, for in it, as in the sea and all nature, he seems to sense the basic beat of life, health, and regeneration. His voice carries a musical undertone. It is as naked and sincere as his emotions. Only Phineas has what to Gene is a "shocking self-acceptance" (p. 7). Only Phineas never really lies.

At the beginning of the book Phineas sets the stage for his own special function. On forcing Gene out of the tree for the first time, he says, "I'm good for you that way. You tend to back away otherwise" (p. 9). Phineas knows that Gene must jump from the tree, because in some cryptic fashion which only he seems to understand, they are "getting ready for the war" (p. 14). Among the Devon boys only Phineas knows that they must be conforming in every possible way to what is happening and what is going to happen in the general warfare of life. The first necessary step toward successful confrontation of what is going to happen rests in self-knowledge.

One cold winter morning, after Finny's "accident," Gene is running a large circle around Phineas, being trained, as Phineas puts it, for the 1944 Olympic Games. With his broken leg Phineas knows that the Games are closed to himself; he will have to participate through Gene, who was always as disinterested in sports as Phineas seemed to be in his studies. Gene is huffing, his body and lungs wracked with tiring pains that hit like knife thrusts. "Then," he says, "for no reason at all, I felt magnificent. It was as though my body until that instant had simply been lazy, as though the aches and exhaustion were all imagined, created from nothing in order to keep me from truly exerting myself. Now my body seemed at last to say, 'Well, if you must have it, here!' and an accession of strength came flooding through me. Buoyed up, I forgot my usual feeling of routine self-pity when working out, I lost myself, oppressed mind along with aching body; all entanglements were shed, I broke into the clear" (p. 105). After finishing the grueling run Gene and his Olympian coach have the following significant and two-leveled conversation:

Phineas: You found your rhythm, didn't you, that third time around. Just as you came into that straight part there.
Gene: Yes, right there.
Phineas: You've been pretty lazy all along, haven't you?

Gene: Yes, I guess I have been.
Phineas: You didn't even know anything about yourself.
Gene: I don't guess I did, in a way (p. 106).

At one point Gene decides that Phineas' seemingly irrepressible mind (he ignored many of the small rules of behavior at Devon) was not completely unleashed, that he did abide by certain rules of conduct "cast in the form of Commandments" (p. 25). One rule is that you should not lie. Another is that one should always pray because there just might be a God. And there is the idea that is the key to the entire Phineas outlook: that "You always win at sports" (p. 25). To Phineas, sports were the absolute good, the measure of the balanced life. The significance that eludes Gene at this point, as it eludes most people everywhere today, is that everyone *can* and *should* win at sports, because in the Greek view of Phineas sports are not so much a competition against others—a matter of pride and winning at any cost—but a competition against oneself, a healthy struggle in which one measures his capacities without ego, fear, or *hubris*. We easily identify with Gene's total disbelief when Phineas privately shatters a school swimming record but wishes no public recognition. He says, "I just wanted to see if I could do it. Now I know" (p. 34). This is the Olympic Games spirit as it should be and as it perhaps once was. Phineas adds, "when they discovered the circle they created sports" (p. 27). And when they discovered the circle they also created the universal symbol for the whole man.

Using classical myth as a tool for understanding the present is hardly new to literature. James Joyce, for one, demonstrated with genius its relevance to modern life and art. In *A Separate Peace*, myth is molded and altered when necessary to fit Knowles' dramatic purposes. The episode concerning the Devon Winter Carnival, that special artistic creation of Phineas, not only provides excellent examples of Knowles' mythological method, but is thematically very important as marking the symbolic point of passage for the Olympic spirit—its flame of life—from Phineas to Gene. It is during the carnival scene that Phineas, leg in cast, dances a rapturous and wild bacchanal, his special, and last, "choreography of peace" (p. 120). For the briefest of moments in a drab world's drabbest season Phineas creates a world of Dionysian celebration that infuses Gene with divine enthusiasm. At this point, Knowles chooses to blend the figure of the young Phoebus Apollo (Phineas before the fall) with that of the resurrected Dionysus (Phineas after his fall; who has finally discovered what "suffering" is) (p. 101).

In ancient Greece the Dionysian festival began in the spring of the year with Greek women travelling into the hills to be "reborn" again through mystical union with the God of Wine. They danced, they drank, they leaped in wild frenzy as all restraint melted away. At the center of the ceremony they seized a goat, perhaps a bull, sometimes a man (all believed to be incarnations of Dionysus), and tore the live victim to shreds. A ceremony of pagan communion followed in which the victim's blood was quaffed and the flesh eaten, whereby the communicants thought their souls would be entered and possessed by their resurrected god. Knowles surely bore in mind the festival of Dionysus when erecting his superb carnival scene. In a sense, this invention of Phineas marks his resurrection, for it is the first project in which he has exhibited personal interest since his fall. At last, though briefly, the "old" Phineas seems to have returned somewhat in body and spirit. Amid a scene of mayhem, in which "there was going to be no government, even by whim" (p. 119), the boys circle around Brinker Hadley, throw themselves upon him, and forcibly take his jealously guarded cache of hard cider. They drink, they dance, they throw off the fear and "violence latent in the day" (p. 119), losing themselves completely in the festival of Phineas. Then, with the burning of Homer's book of war, *The Iliad*, a specialized version of the Olympic Games begins, a somewhat nicer type of "warfare." Soon, from the monarch's chair of black walnut—whose regal legs and arms end in the paws and heads of lions—Phineas rises to full height on the prize table, and at the "hub" (p. 116) of the proceedings begins his wild bacchanal. Gene says that "Under the influence not I know of the hardest cider but of his own inner joy at life for a moment as it should be, as it was meant to be in his nature, Phineas recaptured that magic gift for existing primarily in space, one foot conceding briefly to gravity its rights before spinning him off again into the air. It was his wildest demonstration of himself, of himself in the kind of world he loved; it was his choreography of peace" (p. 120).

Prior to the Carnival, Gene says he had acted simply as a "Chorus" (p. 119) to Phineas, but now the beautiful boy-god, sitting amid the tabled prizes, makes a request of Gene: on a physical level, to qualify for their Olympic Games; on a spiritual level, to qualify for salvation. During the past weeks Gene has made the Phineas outlook and spirit more and more a part of his own, and so infused, he now reacts to the request in the only way possible: ". . . it wasn't cider which made me in this moment champion of everything he ordered, to run as though I were the abstraction of speed, to walk the half-circle of statues on my hands, to balance on my head on top of the icebox on top of the Prize Table, to jump if he had asked it across the Naguamsett and land crashing in the middle of Quackenbush's boat house, to accept at the end of it amid a clatter of applause—for this day even the schoolboy egotism of Devon was conjured away—a wreath made from the evergreen trees which Phineas placed on my head" (pp. 120–21).

Somehow, Gene has mystically been passed the saving spirit and code of Phineas. His new growth and knowledge are immediately tested. The Carnival ends prematurely when Gene receives an ominous telegram from Leper Lepellier asking Gene to come to his winter-bound home in Vermont. Gene suspects that the fruits of such an isolated meeting will not be pleasant ones, but he also knows that he must sometimes face certain harsh realities alone, even if only a little at a time. Also, he realizes that he has a chance to endure now, for the influence of Phineas, god of sun, light, and truth, is always with him. As he finally approaches Leper's house he thinks that, like Phineas, "The sun was the blessing of the morning, the one celebrating element, an aesthete with no purpose except to shed radiance. Everything else was sharp and hard, but this *Grecian sun* (my italics) evoked joy from every angularity and blurred with brightness the stiff face of the countryside. As I walked briskly out the road the wind knifed at my face, but this sun caressed the back of my neck" (p. 124).

Now Gene does not immediately dash away when learning the grim tale of Leper's Section-Eight. The summer before Gene would have run quickly from such unpleasantness back to the maternal and more secure confines of old Devon, but now he needs "too much to know the facts," (p. 129) and though he finally does run away in the "failing sunshine" (p. 130) from the horrible details of Leper's casualty, he has shown strong signs of significant progress. "I had had many new experiences," Gene says, "and I was growing up" (p. 140).

Physically, Phineas dies. The reasons are twofold. All gods must die physically; it is in their nature to be spiritual, and in the case of many, sacrificial. Phineas dies that Gene might live. Second, Phineas must be crushed physically to emphasize that the present world is really no place for the full-blown powers and principles which he represents in his symbolic guise of Phoebus Apollo. Changes in man's psychological makeup do not erupt like some overnight volcano of the sea. Such transition is always painfully slow, necessarily too slow. But perhaps now, in a ruptured world that is heaped with war's unromantic statistics and computerized cruelties, humanity will choose to reemerge from its emotional rubble. Gene always had the brilliance, the IQ, the "brains," but they were untempered by a proper emotional stance. He had envy and he had great fear. He had no balance. Phineas disappears in a physical sense, but his spiritual influence, a portion of his code, will endure in Gene—a tiny spark in the darkness searching for human tinder. The spirit of Apollo has possessed its prophet and will now speak through his mouth. Gene's self has become "Phineas-filled" (p. 185), and to Gene, Phineas was "present in every moment of every day" (p. 184) since he died. First Gene and then perhaps a few others will relearn the road to Greece. "I was ready for the war," Gene says, "now that I no longer had any hatred to contribute to it. My fury was gone, I felt it gone, dried up at the source, withered and lifeless. Phineas had absorbed it and taken it with him, and I was rid of it forever" (p. 185). Even fifteen years later when Gene returns to Devon he approaches the school down a street lined with houses to him reminiscent of "Greek Revival temples" (p. 2). The cause of wars within and without the individual, that "something ignorant in the human heart," (p. 183) has now been exorcised.

The purgated emotions of negative content had been fear, jealousy, and hate, emotions which result in wars both personal and global. The positive emotions which then must replace them are friendship, loyalty, and love toward all mankind and nature, emotions which result in peace and an appreciation of life and its beauty. Even though Phineas had broken every minor and stuffy Devon regulation, never had a student seemed to love the school more "truly and deeply" (p. 15). Edith Hamilton writes in *The Greek Way* that "To rejoice in life, to find the world beautiful and delightful to live in, was a mark of the Greek spirit which distinguished it from all that had gone before. It is a vital distinction." So although the world is not yet ready for the apotheosis of some golden Greek Apollo, perhaps it is prepared, after its most recent blood gluts and promises of human extinction, for the first faltering step toward a world full of the Phineas-filled, a step which must necessarily begin with the conquering of a small part of the forest of self—a step toward the far frontiers of ancient Greece.

Paul Witherington on the Novel's Structure

There is something almost diabolical about Finny's "innocence." His power over people is uncanny; Gene describes it as hypnotic, and it consists of inducing others temporarily to suspend their practical, logical systems of belief to follow his non-logical argument, acted out either verbally or on the playing fields. The answers he gives in class are "often not right but could rarely be branded as wrong" (p. 64), for they presuppose a world in which ordinary standards of judgment are impossible. Finny's pranks themselves—skipping classes and meals, wearing the school tie as a belt, playing poker in the dorm—are actually serious offenses only within the disciplinary framework of a prep school. The audacity is his defense of them which is always disconcerting because it is never relevant, or sometimes too relevant, as when he is being frank about a normally touchy subject. Finny's simplicity, by its very rarity, tends to shock and to threaten the established order of things, to throw ordinary people off balance.

Further ambiguity exists in the imagery of flow which Knowles uses to describe Finny's harmony with others and with his environment. Friendship to Finny is a harmony of equal tensions and movements. Like his idea that everybody always wins at sports, this notion of reciprocal benevolence naively presupposes a level of human interaction superior not only to individual selfishness but also to pressures and events of the actual world. "When you really love something, then it loves you back," he tells Gene (p. 136), but when Finny confesses his feelings for Gene on the beach, Gene is too embarrassed to answer. Finny cannot understand why people build walls between what they feel and what they let others know they feel; his benevolence, a two-way avenue between friends, is his reason for being. His walk, his play and even his body itself are described as a flow, a harmony within and without, a primitive attunement to natural cycles. The world of graduation, the draft, and adult necessity is oriented differently, however, and Finny's rhythm is broken in his fall into the civilized world: "There was an interruption, brief as a drum beat, in the continuous flow of his walk, as though with each step he forgot for a split-second where he was going" (p. 191). After Finny's second fall, on the stairs, he dies when bone marrow gets in the bloodstream and stops his heart.

Yet Knowles is careful not to oversimplify nor to sentimentalize Finny's stopped flow, the heart ruptured by a violent world. Like the Devon River, that clear, innocent center of summer fun in which the boys play their last summer of childhood, Finny is shut off from natural progress, dammed into isolation and perpetual youth. Below the dam the Naguamsett River, center of winter activity and symbolic setting of Gene's "baptism" into the world of adulthood, is "ugly, saline, fringed with marsh, mud and seaweed" (p. 91), but it does flow into the world-encircling sea to be influenced by the Gulf Stream, the Polar Ice Cap, and the moon; like Gene it, eventually, after some difficulty, involves itself in world movements. The Devon and Finny are relics of some earlier, less complex era, self-sufficient but out of the flow of time, able to give rise and even direction to the stream of mankind, but themselves unable to follow into a mature involvement. There is irony in the fact that Gene's rigid, West Point stride endures, whereas Finny's graceful body breaks so easily; of course Finny risks much more, for his position is supported precariously by shaky illusions. Like Billy Budd's stutter which seems aggravated in the moments when he confronts evil in the world and has no adequate language to express his feelings about it, Finny's flawed flow steadily becomes worse with each new awareness of the hate around him.

Finally, love and hate are themselves ambiguous in *A Separate Peace*, from Gene's first suspicions of an undercurrent of rivalry till the time in the army when he wonders if the "enemy" he killed at Devon was really an enemy at all. Gene is never sure of his relationship with Finny because he—like the reader who sees the action through Gene's eyes—is never sure what Finny represents, whether he is a well-meaning friend who simply resists growing up, a pernicious fraud acting out of spite, or a neurotic who builds protective illusions. . . .

For Finny, life is a continuous effort to control reality by creating comfortable myths about it. War is only make-believe on the fields and rivers of Devon: a game resembling football and soccer is invented and named, for its speed and devastating unpredictability, "blitzball;" snowball fights are staged as military operations; the tree hanging over the Devon River is a torpedoed ship that must be evacuated. But these games which at first seem to have the practical function of preparing boys mentally and physically for war actually become shields against reality, ways of sugarcoating the externals of war by making its participants invulnerable, like playful Olympian deities. Finny is unable to distinguish between playing and fighting, the forms of which seem similar within his romantic, naive frame of reference. Like his theory of reciprocal benevolence, his theory of games is based on the assumption that what *should be* true *can be* once the proper pattern is erected. It is true that Finny is a superb athlete who usually wins any physical contest, and it is also true that Finny often defines winning and losing—the rules of the game itself—during play, but the real basis for Finny's notion that everybody always wins at sports is his idea that the game consists in finding a proper method of play which then makes its outcome irrelevant. His rigidity in this respect is most apparent in a game he plays badly, poker. Following a plan that ought to win, Finny ignores the fact that he actually never does, even when the game is his own weird invention, like a child who asks and keeps asking a question, learning the language by which to frame it and seeming not to hear the answer that is given.

Finny appears essential to Devon's organized defense against war, not only because he directs the boys' last peaceful summer of play and infuses it with ideals of love and equal interaction, but because he seems to have the power to sustain this idyllic atmosphere beyond its natural limits. Described by Gene, Finny is a primitive, god-like priest celebrating the essential unity and indestructibility of man and nature and mediating between the two: "Phineas in exaltation, balancing on one foot on the prow of a canoe like a river god, his raised arms invoking the air to support him, face transfigured, body a complex set of balances and compensations, each muscle aligned in perfection with all the others to maintain this supreme fantasy of achievement, his skin glowing from immersions, his whole body hanging between river and sky as though he had transcended gravity and might by gently pushing upward with his foot glide a little way higher and remain suspended in space, encompassing all the glory of the summer and offering it to the sky" (p. 90). Even after he falls from the tree, Finny preserves this function as priest. His broken body makes winter seem inevitable but only temporary, and his creation of the winter carnival by fiat ["And because it was Finny's idea, it happened as he said" (p. 160)] is an act of magic designed to recreate the harmony of summer. The ritual is begun by burning the *Iliad*, not so much as a protest against war as a magical attempt to destroy war by destroying an early, typical account of it. Standing on a table at the ceremonies, hopping about on his one good leg in protest against war and deformity, Finny tries to represent life as he feels it should be; the others, intoxicated with their desire for earlier, less demanding forms of existence, allow Finny to lead them in this "choreography of peace" (p. 169), suggesting Hart Crane's line in *The Bridge*: "Lie to us—dance us back the tribal morn."

In Finny's universe all things are possible as long as the bulwark of illusion holds; as long as Finny can believe each morning, for example, that his leg has overnight been miraculously healed, there is evidence for all magic, not only his but that of a sympathetic universe. When reality does not meet his expectations, though, he is gradually forced into a defensive position. At Gene's "trial" by fellow students, Finny testifies that he believed the tree itself shook him out and tumbled him to the ground. This is more than a defense of Gene, just as the "trial" is more than Gene's; it is Finny's defense of himself, of his notions of reciprocal benevolence and of the inner harmony of all things, and of that supernatural world which sustains these illusions. The evidence convicts him as well as Gene, but—as his second fall shows—Finny cannot adapt to the fact of a Darwinian universe, a world where there are no absolute principles, but only the reality met in experience. The danger of building unsupportable myths like Finny's is shown in Knowles' second novel *Morning in Antibes* (1962); Nick, the central character, in a state of agony at losing his own hold on reality, "spontaneously" composes a poem illustrating his condition:

> The tightrope walker is tired
> Because he must always lean forward
> To weave the rope
> (*Morning in Antibes*, p. 168)

The fall comes—as in so many movie cartoons—not when one does the impossible, but when one realizes that he is doing what in fact is impossible. Finny dies when he realizes he has had no magic, that he can no longer, as Knowles puts it, exist "primarily in space" (p. 169). The other boys are propelled forward into the real world by the force of Finny's violent death, for spring inexorably comes in spite of his physical decay, and the correspondence between the priest and the object of his religion is broken.

Finny's imagination moves always from war to play, first grasping the game as a simile for war and then—when the thought of training for something which he cannot use becomes unendurable—playing the game as a substitute for war. The imaginations of the other boys move in opposite directions, from play to war, for that is the way of growing up, recognizing that the patterns of childhood are masks behind which stand the real patterns of life. One day at Devon these different imaginations, facing opposite directions, reach a high moment of dramatic tension in a mock snow war that prefigures Finny's death: "We ended the fight in the only way possible; all of us turned on Phineas. Slowly, with a steadily widening grin, he was driven down beneath a blizzard of snowballs" (p. 192). Afterwards on the way back to the gym, Finny remarks that it was a good, funny fight. Gene does not answer; he has for some time had conscious premonitions about things to come, about a turned-inside-out situation where games become real wars: "I didn't trust myself in them, and I didn't trust anyone else. It was as though football players were really bent on crushing the life out of each other, as though boxers were in combat to the death, as though even a tennis ball might turn into a bullet" (p. 102). This is a prelude to the awareness that world wars are but expansions of individual hatred and ignorance and therefore anticlimactic to the anguish of growing up. For Gene the war with Germany and Japan is a simile for his experiences at Devon, less intense because less personal.

The ability to see patterns between world wars and personal wars and between friendly and hostile conflict is to see at once the horrible depravity and the irony of the world where varying and even conflicting experiences often take on the same form. This consciousness of ambiguity, this appreciation of the variety and relativity of human experience, is what Gene learns. His movement, in short, is not toward the primitive, magical effort to control reality in the sense of making it fit preconceived ideas but toward the naturalistic effort to understand reality by relating it to forms of personal experience. As the patterns of experience are realized, they take on meaning, and this meaning itself is a kind of control, not that of the magician but of the artist who finds order and harmony in the structure of things rather than in categorical moral imperatives.

Rejecting Finny's magical view promotes in Gene a new awareness of self and a new self-responsibility. As the compulsive rituals of Finny give way to Gene's nonprescriptive view, and myth is conceived as serving experience rather than dictating it, Gene separates himself from his environment and recognizes in himself the capabilities for idealism and hatred he had formerly projected on the outside world. This emancipation is represented symbolically in Gene's changing relationship with Finny. At first he thinks of himself, rather guiltily, as an extension of Finny, but after becoming an athlete in his own right he sees Finny as smaller, both relatively and absolutely, like memories from childhood, like the tree at Devon which seemed "high as a beanstalk" and yet is scarcely recognizable years later. Finally Gene thinks of himself as including Finny ("Phineas-filled"), and this indicates his maturity: preserving the myth associated with Finny but only so it can serve him as it serves the artist, as a metaphor for experience.

Finny tries to construct a separate peace by explaining away the war as a fraud or by ignoring its content of violence, and Knowles' message is, of course, that this is impossible. Much as Finny's ideal world of changelessness, irresponsibility, and illusion is desirable—and Knowles does present it as desirable—one must eventually abandon it for the world of possibility. Gene's final comment, made on his return to Devon years after the major action of the novel, is the key to what he has learned from the tragedy of Finny: "Nothing endures, not a tree, not love, not even a death by violence. Changed, I headed back through the mud. I was drenched; anybody could see it was time to come in out of the rain" (p. 11). Gene frees himself from fear not by hiding from war and the ambiguities of the human heart, not by building barriers between youth and age, but by accepting the inevitability of change and loss. The act of coming in out of the rain, that ancient criterion distinguishing the idealist from the realist, represents the peace Gene finds, the treaty established between what the world should be and what it really is.

JAMES L. McDONALD ON KNOWLES'S CONTEXT AND INFLUENCES

It may be too early to attempt more than a tentative appraisal of the overall achievement of John Knowles. Certainly one can say that he ranks among the most promising young American novelists; and one can recognize the obvious fact that *A Separate Peace* (winner of the William Faulkner Foundation Award and the Rosenthal Award) has become a small classic among college students and seems likely to last for some time. His other novels, however, have only been noticed in passing: *Morning in Antibes* and *Indian Summer* have not really been analyzed and evaluated. Nor is there any substantial critical commentary on Knowles's work as a whole.

I would like to begin such a commentary; and I propose to do so by placing Knowles, as it were—by relating him to the American literary tradition which I see him working within. He is writing what Lionel Trilling has called "the novel of manners"; and it seems to me that there are affinities between his aesthetic preoccupations and those of Henry James and F. Scott Fitzgerald. An examination of his subjects, themes, and techniques should show this affinity; and I hope that it will also provide a basis for a reasonably sound estimate of Knowles's stature as a novelist.

From the beginning of his career, Knowles—like James and Fitzgerald—has written about manners, about what Trilling defines as "a culture's hum and buzz of implication . . . the whole evanescent context in which its explicit statements are made." In Knowles's first novel, *A Separate Peace* (New York, 1959), the "explicit statements" are the Second World War and its moral effect on American society; the "context" is made up of the precarious situation of American prep-school students who will soon be combatants, and of the moral responses that they, their teachers, and their parents make to this situation.

As many critics have noted, *A Separate Peace* can be viewed as a war novel, drawing its title from Frederic Henry's personal declaration of personal armistice in *A Farewell to Arms*. Knowles's concern, however, is not with the direct confrontation of the obvious realities of the battlefield; rather, it is with the impact of war on the minds and sensibilities of individuals who are not, as yet, immediately involved. The novel examines the cultural upheaval created by the war, and shows how the resulting moral climate affects the thoughts, feelings, attitudes, and actions of Gene Forrester, Phineas, Leper, Brinker, and the others. The novel deals, then, with culture, and with the sensibility of the individual as it is formed by a particular culture; like James and Fitzgerald, Knowles draws the reader's attention to the individual's efforts to adjust to cultural change, and to the quality of his moral responses as he attempts to cope with the disruption of his formerly stable world.

Particularly Jamesian in this novel is Knowles's use of point of view. The narrator, the principal character, is Gene Forrester. On the surface, it appears that he is telling his story honestly, attempting to grapple with his past and forthrightly informing the reader of its significance. Yet, like the narrators of James's "The Liar" or *The Aspern Papers*, for example, Forrester frequently seems either unaware of or deliberately unwilling to acknowledge the moral nature and consequences of his attitudes and actions. There is, then, a discrepancy between Forrester's judgments and the actions and attitudes he is judging. The reader's awareness of this discrepancy is enforced by the dramatic statements of other characters in the novel, especially by the comments of Leper.

Thus the reader's judgments are not always the same as the narrator's; and so the reader is led to question the narrator's motives and interpretations. Should Forrester be taken at his own evaluation? Or is he really, as Leper charges, "a savage underneath" his pose of refined, dispassionate, reflective survivor and recounter of the ordeal?

The complexity—or the ambiguity—of the novel is precisely here, and so is Knowles's debt to James. Neither novelist merely uses his narrator to direct the narrative. Both, instead, use the narrative as the scene and occasion of a complex, dramatic confrontation between the narrator and his past which the reader participates in. For James and Knowles, the aesthetic effect of this type of novel depends on a dramatic interplay between the narrator's judgments and the reader's; and, in this sense, the narrator is the story.

JAMES M. MELLARD ON VISION AND COUNTERPOINT IN THE NOVEL

Arising naturally from setting, the novel's contrapuntal symbolism operates organically in the development of its theme, the growth to maturity through the loss of adolescent innocence and the acceptance of adult experience. The basic symbolism is the contrast between the peace of the school and the war going on outside, for it provides the objective correlative for the subjective battles fought by the youthful characters as they search for personal fulfillment. It is against the war, therefore, that Gene Forrester, the central and point-of-view character of the novel, directs most of his thoughts. To Gene, "The war was and is reality"; and for much of the novel, it is the hard world of reality, of the war, that Gene, at times only unconsciously, hopes to evade, a desire he manages to fulfill, during most of the final school year, through the intervention of his friend Phineas, or "Finny," as he is usually called. Gene says, for example, that "the war swept over like a wave at the seashore, gathering power and size as it bore on us, overwhelming in its rush, seemingly inescapable, and then at the last moment eluded by a word from Phineas. . . ." Yet the war, like growth and maturity, can hardly be avoided forever, because "one wave is inevitably followed by another even larger and more powerful, when the tide is coming in." So the youths at Devon, and particularly Gene, enjoy their "momentary, illusory, special and separate peace" whenever they can, just as, during Devon's first Summer Session, the faculty relaxed its controls on the boys because they "reminded them of what peace was like."

The fundamental counterpoint between war and peace, reality and illusion, is made more immediate in the symbolic contrast between the "gypsy" summer and the "unromantic" winter. Members of the only summer session in Devon's history, Gene, Phineas and the others make the best of it, managing to break most of the school's rules while still maintaining the faculty's good will, playing at warfare, making up chaotic new games, such as "Blitzball," and forming new clubs, like the "Super Suicide Society of the Summer Session." Supporting the contrast between the reality of the war and the illusions of peace, the opposition between summer and winter is essentially a balancing of the world of fantasy, dream, and desire against the world of fact, even of nightmare and repulsion. As long as the summer lasts, the sense of peace and fulfillment and happiness conquers the encroachments of the war, with its defeats, frustrations and pain: "Bombs in Central Europe were completely unreal to us here, not because we couldn't imagine it . . . but because our place here was too fair for us to accept something like that. . . ." But just as another wave will follow the one eluded, the Winter Session will replace the Summer Session: "It had been the school's first, but this was its one hundred and sixty-third Winter Session, and the forces assembled for it scattered the easygoing summer spirit like so many fallen leaves." At the first Chapel, of the new session, Gene thinks how Devon had changed during the summer, how "traditions had been broken, the standards let down, all rules forgotten," but he also realizes that the summer is past, that retribution awaits:

Ours had been a wayward gypsy music, leading us down
all kinds of foolish gypsy ways, unforgiven. I was glad

of it. I had almost caught the rhythm of it, the dancing, clicking jangle of it during the summer.

Still it had come to an end, in the last long rays of daylight at the tree, when Phineas fell. It was forced upon me as I sat chilled through the Chapel service, that this probably vindicated the rules of Devon after all, wintery Devon. If you broke the rules, then they broke you. That, I think, was the real point of the sermon on this first morning.

And at this juncture, with school beginning, the summer over, Phineas gone and unlikely to return because of a shattered leg, and the too, too real world of the war reasserting itself, Gene gives himself to the disturbing thought that the "idiosyncratic, leaderless band" of the summer would soon be back under the control of the "official class leaders and politicians." But because the "gypsy days" had intervened and he had absorbed much from Finny, Gene attempts to fight the world alone, a personal battle doomed to failure, but which has momentary triumphs after Finny returns to guide him. The climax of this battle, the "Winter Carnival," is itself a result of the contrast between winter and summer and Gene's desire to restore the spirit of the past summer in the dead of winter. "On this Saturday at Devon," Gene says, "there was going to be no government," and "on this day even the schoolboy egotism of Devon was conjured away." At the Winter Carnival, just before the news of Leper's army desertion, Gene comes closest to regaining the summer place beside his friend Phineas. But this idyllic interlude is followed immediately by Gene's journey through the demonic wintry wasteland of northern New England to see Leper, a trip which reasserts the fact of the war.

Another use of counterpoint and one even more specific than the seasonal symbolism is the antithesis between the two rivers that run through the Devon campus and that make the school itself part of the dualistic symbolism. As the summer connotes peace and dream and fantasy, the Devon River represents goodness, beauty, even purity: "going into the Devon was like taking a refreshing shower itself, you never had to clean up after it." It is associated with the cultivated, the pastoral, the idyllic, with the "familiar hills," the "highland farms and forests we knew." The "turbid" Naguamsett, associated with winter, suggests everything contrary to the spirit of the Devon: it is "ugly, saline, fringed with marsh," and it is "governed by unimaginable factors." But as the war overtakes peace, and winter replaces summer, the highland Devon must drop into the lowland Naguamsett, a vicissitude which suggests once again that youth cannot avoid the responsibilities of maturity. So, if the events of the "gypsy summer" take place beside and in the Devon, the events of the winter must take place beside and in the Naguamsett. And where the central image of the summer is Gene and his "best pal" Phineas leaping together into the Devon, in a gesture of brotherhood, the key image of the winter session is Gene and Quackenbush catapulting into the Naguamsett, "in the middle of a fight."

In addition to the symbolic counterpoint arising from the temporal and physical settings, contrapuntal character relationships control the development of theme and structure. The major character conflict is that which Gene imagines to exist between him and Finny. Like the novel's symbolism, this conflict grows rather naturally from the setting, for a sense of rivalry often prevails in such schools as Devon. Superficially, it is based upon the school's dual emphasis on athletics and scholarship, because Finny is by far the school's best athlete, while Gene is close to being its very best student. Once Gene decides that they are rivals and that Finny has been artfully concealing his ambitions and attempting to wreck his studies, he decides that they are enemies as well, and, like it or not, they "are even in enmity." But the conflict between Finny and Gene goes much deeper than this, for there are essential oppositions in personality. The fundamental contrast is simply that Gene is all too human and heir to all the weaknesses of flesh and spirit, while Finny, at least as Gene sees him most of the time, is little less than a divinity. Thus where Gene is at times morally and ethically shallow, Finny is the epitome of honesty and openness and fidelity. And yet, of the two, Finny is the nonconformist, for his values are generally self-created, although they never seem self-interested. Thus Gene says,

> ... I noticed something about Finny's own mind, which was such an opposite from mine. It wasn't completely unleashed after all. I noticed that he did abide by certain rules, which he seemed to cast in the form of commandments. "Never say you are five feet nine when you are five feet eight and a half" was the first one I encountered. Another was, "Always say some prayers at night because it might turn out there is a God."

This last "Commandment" is a good illustration of the quality of Finny's mind, for it in no way represents a self-protective covering of his bets; on the contrary, it shows Finny's desire to see the world as it ought to be; hence Gene's memories are of "Phineas losing even in those games he invented, betting always for what *should* win, for what would have been the most brilliant successes of all, if only the cards hadn't betrayed him." Gene, on the other hand, usually played conservatively, aware at all times of percentages, rules, conventions; consequently, to Gene one of the most astounding of Finny's feats is not so much his breaking a school swimming record without a day of practice, but his unwillingness to have it publicized or even officially recognized, for what Gene values most, at least in the beginning, is conventional and public approval. Thus while Finny has relative values, Gene's values are absolute; where "Finny's life was ruled by inspiration and anarchy," Gene's "was subject to the dictates of [his] own mind, which gave [him] the maneuverability of a strait jacket." And where Finny is the "essence of ... peace," freedom, courage and selflessness, Gene, until he becomes, as it were, a part of Finny, is swayed by some "ignorance" inside him and trapped by his own guilt and fear and egotism.

Although Knowles insists upon the contrasts between Finny and Gene, he also shows that the two antithetical personalities can, even must, merge into one, just as summer slides into winter, the Devon into the Naguamsett, peace into war. But if these changes seem to be governed by something absolute and unfathomable and yet seem to create something better out of a process that appears undesirable, Gene's transformation also seems to result in a being of greater durability, if not of goodness, one better able to keep his balance in a chaotic world than either the original Gene or Finny. To Gene, Finny is a god, a god of the river, as his name suggests. But, god or man, Finny is not, as Gene tells him, suited for the world as it is, for the war and, thus, for reality. Hence, Phineas, besides his initial contrast to Gene, even points to a strong contrapuntal character symbolism: both the representative of Gene's "fall from innocence" and grace and the means for his deliverance and redemption, in a novel filled with Christian symbols and a theme linked to the concepts of original sin and the fortunate fall, Phineas becomes both Adam and Christ, the "second Adam," in a concentrated, powerful symbolism that is paradoxical, but also traditionally Christian. And, "Phineas-filled" at the novel's conclusion, Gene is enabled to size up the world, like Phineas, "with erratic and entirely personal reservations, letting its rocklike facts sift through and be accepted only a little at a time, only as much as he could assimilate without a sense of chaos and loss."

The uses of counterpoint in symbolism and characterization are important, but they by no means complete *A Separate Peace*. Of equal significance are the contrapuntal devices of plot and structure. There are many actions that have their counteractions in the novel, but the major counterpointed scenes are those that involve Finny's two falls, the markers that determine the three-part structure of the novel. As in symbolism and characterization, the structure of the novel shows a kind of dialectical movement, first revealing the antitheses between the two central figures, then suggesting the "transformation" of one, Gene, into his opposite, and finally portraying, in dramatically convincing ways, the reconciliation of the opposites into one unified, complete and well adjusted personality, who, better than most, can come to terms with the dual attractions of the world.

The climax of part one, at the end of Chapter Four, is the fall of Phineas from the tree beside the Devon River, but it is prepared for by Gene's increasing suspicions and sense of rivalry. Gene's erroneous but nevertheless powerful distrust of Finny begins to emerge when he watches a sunrise at the beach, after Finny had inveigled him to skip school; it culminates when Gene, in a realization that "broke as clearly and bleakly as dawn at the beach," decides that his friend "had deliberately set out to wreck" his studies so that they would not be even. Shortly after, however, at the tree where the "Suicide Society" members test their devotion to the club, Gene recognizes his tremendous spiritual isolation and physical fear, for, although he cannot yet understand why, he realizes that Finny "had never been jealous . . . for a second." So now he realizes more than ever that he "was not of the same quality" as Phineas, a "truth," however, that he cannot abide at all. Moments later, Gene shakes the limb on which they are balancing and causes Finny to fall. The counterpart to this scene of "crime," at the center of which is a ritual test of personal and idiosyncratic values, is the scene of "punishment," the trial that precedes the second fall at the end of Chapter Eleven. The trial reverses the implications of the first fall, for it indicates Gene's progress away from isolation toward social integration.

Just as the scenes preceding the falls are contrasted, the results of the falls are also carefully counterpointed. The major contrast is in the reversal of the influences upon Gene and Phineas: the first fall is far more important to Gene than to Finny, for while it causes physical anguish for Finny, it creates a much greater emotional anguish for Gene. His anguish releases him from fear, but it creates a social guilt and alienation and a corresponding need to identify completely with Phineas, to "become" Phineas, as it were, in order to escape himself. But as Gene grows more and more sure of himself, of his own identity and "real authority and worth," he comes to depend less and less upon Phineas, who was, because of his disability, so dependent upon Gene that he thought of Gene as an "extension of himself." Consequently, the second fall has far greater ramifications for Finny than for Gene. After this accident, Finny is forced to acknowledge the existence of "something blind" in man's character and to accept the fact that Gene caused his original fall because of "some kind of blind impulse." If the ultimate effect of the two falls upon Gene was to make him more capable of existing in the "real" world, their contrary effect upon Finny was simply to destroy him: as Gene had told him long before, Phineas was "too good to be true," so there really could be no place in the world for him, no matter how hard he or Gene might wish it.

Although Phineas is its most memorable character, *A Separate Peace* is Gene's story, and the point of that story is Gene's growing into maturity and accepting his place in the world. Consequently, the most important scene for Gene, after the falls, is his inevitable but painful recognition of the world's and his own duality. This recognition involves the contrast of his youthful, adolescent, "old" way of viewing the world with a more mature, adult, "new" way. Occurring just after Phineas' accident on the stairs, in the building where "boys come to be made men," this scene is the literal and symbolic aftermath of Finny's rejection of Gene. It is actually the climax of the novel because Gene's emotional rejection of Finny's way of life is more important than Finny's death; it shows Gene taking a midnight walk through the campus and sleeping overnight in the stadium. During his walk, Gene says, "I was trying to cope with something that might be called double vision. I saw the gym in the glow of a couple of outside lights near it and I knew of course that it was the Devon gym which I entered every day. It was and it wasn't. There was something innately strange about it, as though there had always been an inner core to the gym which I had never perceived before, quite different from its generally accepted appearance." This "double vision" is true of all else that he sees; everything has a "significance much deeper and far more real than any" he had noticed before, taking on meanings, "levels of reality," he had never suspected. His first impression is that he himself lacked reality, that he was a "ghost," a "dream," a "figment which had never really touched anything." But his real problem as well as his most pressing need are revealed when he says, "I felt that I was not, never had been and never would be a living part of this overpoweringly solid and deeply meaningful world around me."

After the night's sleep in the stadium and the awakening to a fresh new perspective on existence, however, Gene walks back to the "center of the school," has breakfast, gets a notebook from his room and goes to class, actions that suggest powerfully that he has given up Phineas and the stadium, as it were, for his own identity and the classroom. Only now is he enabled again to face Finny with the truth about his first catastrophe and, shortly afterward, to accept, almost without pain, the fact of Finny's death. And it is only after his becoming aware of a double view of reality that Gene steps over the threshold of maturity, now able to recognize existence for what it is, to accept his own position in the world; and to go to war without fear or hatred.

If Phineas has "absorbed" the worst of Gene and taken it with him, Gene has himself absorbed and taken with him the best of Finny—"a way of sizing up the world." Although Gene can "never agree with either" Brinker's or Finny's view of the world ("It would have been comfortable, but I could not believe it."), at least Finny's way of sizing it up with "erratic and entirely personal reservations" allowed one to maintain a coherent, integrated personality. But the key word here is *personal*—one must remain true to himself, his own identity, fulfill his own possibilities rather than another's. So if Gene can never be as innocent as Phineas or regain their "paradise lost," he can at least measure others, as well as himself, against Phineas as he measured the world against Devon, in that prelapsarian summer of 1942. And if he and the others fall short of Finny's standard, as they must, they will still gain from having reached for it.

GORDON E. SLETHAUG ON THE USE OF THE DOUBLE

Through the device of the double, John Knowles in *A Separate Peace* compares two fundamentally different conceptions of the game of life, Gene's, which is a great, hostile and crushingly serious *agon* for domination, and Phineas' which is flippantly playful, truly *paidiac*.

Although this handling of play is unique to *A Separate Peace*, the nature of the double itself follows customary usage. As Milton P. Foster points out, the book shares a common basis with such works as *The Secret Sharer* and *Heart of Darkness* where the narrator is the main character but where the other character, his *alter ego*, occupies most of his thoughts.[3] This view of the second self as a projection of the protagonist's unconscious is fully elaborated both by Otto Rank and Ralph Tymms who see this phenomenon in Freudian terms as Narcissism.[4] In these works, there is a significant sense in which one character parallels or contrasts with another in a deliberate and obvious way, so that the two are seen to be complementary or warring aspects of a central self or identity. In the romances of Conrad these characters may resemble each other, oftentimes exactly although sometimes in fierce opposition, but in more realistic works such as *The Sun Also Rises*, *The Great Gatsby* and *A Separate Peace*, these characters (Jake Barnes and Robert Cohn, Gatsby and Nick, Gene and Finny) will not wholly resemble each other physically but will still have enough affinity that there is no mistaking their relationship nor the resultant implied character-ideal projected by the conflict. In this respect, *A Separate Peace* and these predecessors perfectly illustrate Rank's and Carl Keppler's thesis that the significant literature of the double results from a notion of twinship, either the twin as evil persecutor or beneficent savior.[5] But this book carries the issue even further: Gene is the persecuting double, bent upon his own selfish will to power and desired annihilation of Finny, while Finny is the beneficent double, through his sacrificial death bringing about hope and spiritual growth for Gene. . . .

This conflict is best seen through the characters of Gene and Finny, one from the North and one from the South, who are highlighted against the background of Devon. As their friend Leper notes when seeing them together in the tree before Finny's fall, they "looked as black as—as black as death standing up there with this fire burning all around them" (p. 157). At that moment the two stand virtually indistinguishable and harmonious: neither exists independently of the other. In fact, the purpose of their presence in that fatal tree is to take the "double jump," in which the two boys, identical in age, height and build, are to establish a new record by jumping together. To a great extent, the boys have a special intuitive twin-like rapport, and this jump is designed to cement that bond which has been seen before, for instance when Finny intuitively knows that Gene is afraid to jump, and when he openly expresses admiration for Gene's tan while Gene is secretly admiring his.

This quality of the second self knowing what the first is thinking is one of those attributes of the double tradition, for it marks the inexplicable, almost magical sympathy between the two personalities.[9] At this point in the relationship the bonding of the ludic and agonic is still wholesome. Gene's *agon* has not yet grown uncontrollable, though it will shortly do so. The two tend to be viewed as doubles also by their classmates even after the fall and Finny's disabling, as indicated when Gene applies as assistant manager of the team and Quackenbush refers to him as maimed, and later at the kangaroo court when Brinker snidely comments that Finny seems to have Gene's words in his mouth. Together the two could have been strongly supportive, a blending of highly diverse and contrary elements within human nature, but as they stand, the triumphs and achievements of Finny tend to gall Gene, pushing him toward the precipice of catastrophe that typifies the realistic double.[10] Gene sees Finny as a tempter, while the reader sees Gene as the typically malevolent betraying pursuer of the double tradition. An irrational opposition exists between them even as does an irrational attraction. As is typical of the human context, in this fictional world the polarities are not permitted to merge, blend and unite. Rather, they pull apart, largely due to Gene who sees a growing threat in the person of Finny, even while he is attracted to him and held by their friendship. It is Finny in fact through whom Gene comes to define and understand himself.

The spirit of *paidia*, Phineas is described as a green-eyed, five foot eight and one half inch athletic youth who balances "on one foot on the prow of a canoe like a river god, his . . . body a complex set of balances and compensations, each muscle aligned in perfection with all the others . . . his whole body hanging between river and sky as though he had transcended gravity and might by gently pushing upward with his foot glide a little way higher and remain suspended in space, encompassing all the glory of the summer and offering it to the sky" (p. 63). His combined good looks, fine sense of balance and tremendous energy create the sense of an adamic, unfallen youth or some Dionysus whose physical beauty predates and transcends his twentieth-century context and whose playful attitude has not been corrupted by any negative spirit of competition.[11] His athletic triumphs reinforce this picture, for without much exertion Finny manages to take several prizes for football, hockey and other bodily-contact sports. In one especially telling instance, he swims the pool with only Gene present, earning a better time than the champion swimmer but refusing to divulge the results for public acclaim or to repeat the incident in front of others. He does things for himself, not for public approval and congratulation. In effect, he has no spirit of competition; he simply tests himself within the rules of the game and performs as well as he can. For him the game itself is in most respects his opposing player. He has no particular wish to compete with and win over another person.

When Finny feels that the rules of the game need to be abandoned or changed, he does so with delight for he is not one to be tied to unnecessary and inconsequential rules: he is "a student who combined a calm ignorance of the rules with a winning urge to be good, who seemed to love the school truly and deeply, and never more than when he was breaking the regulations, a model boy who was most comfortable in the truant's corner" (p. 15). In this way he is, as Claire Rosenfield points out, the "good-bad boy" in the sentimental American tradition.[12] When he bends or breaks the rules and shows his unconventionality, he does so with no animosity and so wins others to his opinion, no matter how outrageous the occasion. Only he can with impunity skip dinner after dinner or sleep at the beach when he should be in his room studying. Only he can wear a pink shirt in 1942 and not be called a fairy. And only he can wear the Devon school tie incorrectly as a belt and not be punished by the headmaster. He is equally imaginative and successful in creating his own games and rules. In effect, as the spirit of play, his mind is continually inventive, thinking up new games which will serve as amusement and joy for others. It is he who thinks up the game of Blitzball and the rules for jumping from the trees. Finny is also the one who, even after his leg has been splintered, invents the winter carnival, a sort of boys' school Mardi Gras where invention and chaos take primacy over convention and order. Finny is the spirit of playful inventiveness and freedom from circumscribing rules.

Finny's manic quality extends into every corner of his personality and life. His seemingly careless abandonment of the rules results from a fundamentally spontaneous, antic, Hellenistic nature which is not limited or distorted by sharply defined intellectual or moral prescription. He feels and enjoys without holding his emotions in reserve or fearing the social repercussions of his gaiety. Quite naturally in the midst of his joy, he tells Gene of his affection for him, to which the narrator admits: "It was a courageous thing to say. Exposing a sincere emotion nakedly like that at the Devon School was the next thing to suicide. I should have told him then that he was my best friend also and rounded off what he had said. I started to; I nearly did. But something held me back. Perhaps I was stopped by that level of feeling, deeper than thought, which contains the truth" (p. 38). Gene's level of feeling, deeper than thought, is agonistic, founded on personal antagonism and even sub-conscious dislike. Finny's level of feeling, deeper than thought, is one of complete *joie de vivre*, love and support, whatever the occasion: when Gene lashes out at him for interfering with his studies, Finny is most gracious in backing off; when Gene almost falls out of the tree, Finny risks saving him; when it becomes clear to Finny that Gene has pushed him from the tree, Finny is deeply hurt but ultimately forgiving. His sense of play is morally and physically uplifting for him and others.

Although Finny's self-expression is instinctual and uninhibited by social rules or intellectual restrictions, he is neither morally unconscious nor ignorant. He does nothing dishonest, and he does not lie, never intending deliberately to deceive people or to make himself look good. What may in certain instances seem deceptive is mere playfulness and gamesmanship. Even his declaration that there is no war in Europe is less a stubborn refusal to see reality than a means of sustaining a group joke and snubbing his nose at a war that is radically changing his environment from one of youthful innocence and sportiveness to one of adult experience and cynicism. Of course, his refusal to admit the war into his sphere of reality is also, as he says, a means of protecting his feelings: he desperately wants to participate in this heroic enterprise but is refused because of his splintered leg. Rather than growing negative and bitter, self-accusing and accusing of others, he playfully says there is no war and by that means buoys up his own spirit as well as his classmates'. In short, Finny is an exquisite, unique, prelapsarian youth with "an extra vigor, a heightened confidence in himself, a serene capacity for affection. . . . Nothing as he was growing up at home, nothing at Devon, nothing even about the war had broken his harmonious and natural unity. So [the narrator adds] at last I had" (p. 184). The narrator's tribute to Finny is truly touching, capturing as it does the "liberation we had torn from the gray encroachments of 1943, the escape we had concocted, [the] . . . momentary, illusory, special and separate peace" (p. 121). Finny encapsulates all that is best and highest in youth, all that is possible when filled with the sense of the ludic, and Gene with his guilt-ridden knowledge of having destroyed him represents the tragic vision of conflict that opposes the playful one of comedy and peace.

Although Finny calls Gene his best friend, Gene is unable to return the compliment despite his later coming to realize the inherent value of the relationship. But until just before Finny's death, Gene cannot let go of his opposition to Finny. With his distinctly Spartan sensibility, he *must* see everything as *agon*, as a competition to the death. Finny and Gene are much alike, but at the same time they are polar opposites as much as the Devon and the Naguamsett are physically or as much as Summer differs from Winter. Although the book centers first on Finny (Gene is not even named for the first twenty-seven pages), the reader is always interested in Gene's reaction to Finny because Gene is the narrator and because he obviously has changing reactions to his friend, ranging from love and adulation to envy, mistrust and hate. Of the same height and build as Finny, Gene can wear his clothing. But unlike Finny, Gene is not especially athletic and mistrusts himself and others in sports. He maintains, "I didn't trust myself in them, and I didn't trust anyone else. It was as though football players were really bent on crushing the life out of each other, as though boxers were in combat to the death, as though even a tennis ball might turn into a bullet" (p. 72). For him harmless sports become harmful combats, tennis balls turning into bullets, *paidia* into *agon*.

Consequently, Gene initially considers himself capable of serving only as an assistant team manager, though when Finny later trains him he seems capable of something better. Similarly, he does not have the energy and endurance of Finny and tends to be fearful of jumping out of the tree until Finny shames him into it, fearful of missing dinner or spending an illegal night on the beach, and fearful of dropping an examination. Gene's laurels are not garnered in the world of sports but in academia where he aims to be the best in the class, not just a good student, but an exceptional one. He puts his mind to this task in a cynical way, knowing that his rival, Chet Douglass, is "weakened by the very genuineness of his interest in learning" (p. 44). Gene has no genuine interest in learning but only in becoming the head of the class; his is a single-minded, competitive spirit where he aims not to improve himself and his mind or to test himself against the subject matter, but rather to pit himself against all oncomers, all academic contestants, and to defeat them, to crush the life out of them. Gene lives by his intellect, by his rational side, with the edge of competition sharply honed to keep him in isolation.

Gene feels this competition and rivalry to be quintessential Devon. He notices those instincts in himself, and he attributes them to others as well. So, he aims at being head of the class because he assumes that Finny aims at being the best athlete in order to subvert Gene's own triumph. Early in the summer of '42 he comes to this "realization": "I found it. I found a single sustaining thought. The thought was, You and Phineas are even already. You are even in enmity. You are both coldly driving ahead for yourselves alone. You did hate him for breaking that school swimming record, but so what? He hated you for getting an A in every course but one last term. You would have had an A in that one except for him. Except for him" (p. 43). Furthermore, he says of Finny: ". . . I had detected that Finny's was a den of lonely, selfish ambition. He was no better than I was, no matter who won all the contests" (p. 46). Contrary to what Gene believes or wishes to admit, what he discloses in these thoughts is not Finny's competitive nature but his own because he is a youth who sees everything as competition and rivalry and everyone as an enemy striving to win a battle.

Because Gene regards everyone as a rival or an enemy, he maintains even fifteen years later that "The war was and is reality for me. I still instinctively live and think in its atmosphere" (p. 31). To some extent, Gene's pushing Finny off the branch, setting in motion the circumstances leading to Finny's death, is integrally tied to his own view of life as war. Guiltily, he notes: "I never killed anybody [in the Second World War] and I never developed an intense hatred for the enemy. Because my war ended before I ever put on a uniform; I was on active duty all my time at school; I killed my enemy there" (pp. 185–86). Because Gene perceives his classmates as enemies, he adopts the secretive cunning of a fighter who feels that the game of life does not consist of right or wrong but of the vanquishers and the vanquished, the winners and the losers. He believes that "The thing to be was careful and self-preserving" (p. 143).

He will lie implicitly or explicitly to preserve his image; so, he puts pictures above his bed which will lead people to believe that he is landed gentry from the deep South; and when he is put on trial at the kangaroo court, he lies about not being in the tree when Finny fell so that his crime will not be discovered. He also has a kind of animal cunning which allows him to think that, because Leper has become psychotic and has been given a dishonorable discharge from the war, his testimony against Gene will not be believed by his classmates. Of course, he is wrong about that one, but the incident still illustrates the devious, circumlocutional quality of his mind and morality. Leper, in fact, sees right through him when he remarks: "You always were a lord of the manor, weren't you? A swell guy, except when the chips were down. You always were a savage underneath" (p. 128). . . .

Given his attitude to life as agonistic conflict, ultimately war itself, and his view of ethics as survival tactics, Gene's mode of operation at Devon and his undermining of Finny are characteristic. He is fearful of authorities and does not wish to challenge their rules directly, nor does he wish to lose face with his comrades. He does not want others to know that he is subverting the game's rules, even the game itself. As a result, he often feels caught in a dilemma, caught between supporting the established rules and saving face with Finny who cares little about rules. When faced with that dilemma, he inwardly resents Finny and does his best to subvert him. Even when Finny saves him from falling out of the tree, he is at first thankful and then scornful, first praising and then blaming him. Because Gene cannot learn openness, cannot back away from his rationalized, protective view of life, his jealousy and resentment of Finny grow. Instead of being a "harmonious and natural unity" as is Finny, he becomes fragmented and unnatural. When that unnaturalness and fragmentation intensify, Gene must destroy Finny by pushing him out of the tree; Finny is his rival double that must be destroyed.

The act of pushing Finny has two direct consequences: it makes a cripple of Finny, forcing him to reassess his view of life; and it subjects Gene to a considerable amount of guilt and a new perception of himself in relation to Finny. Physically, Finny's fall is tragic, partially crippling him. Metaphysically, the fall is even more tragic but necessarily human, as was Adam's in eating the fruit or Donatello's of Hawthorne's *Marble Faun* in murdering the model.[15] But the difference in these falls is that Finny is not responsible for his own whereas Adam and Donatello were. Nevertheless, in all cases a new standard of behavior is imposed and a world view revised. Finny is, of course, physically harmed by the fall, his leg splintered in such a way that he cannot participate in sports. His sphere of play is sharply circumscribed. Still, his attitude is, for the most part, one of cheerful optimism. He does not blame Gene, and he continues to laugh and joke.

At certain times, however, he shows a growing negative sensitivity to his wounding; he acknowledges that he now understands the world and human motivation (the fat old men who organize the war) because he has suffered. And some of his jokes have a cynical, cutting edge: there is no war for him because he is crippled and cannot be accepted into the military. Yet, he does not fully suffer until he realizes the extent of Gene's conscious betrayal of him, until he realizes that Gene viewed him as an enemy and pushed him from the tree out of hate, until he realizes that Gene has wantonly destroyed the very game itself. When he comes to the painful awareness that Gene wanted to hurt him, he almost despairs, but Gene's confession to him brings him around once again to an acceptance of their friendship and life, to his belief in the continuing beneficence of their game and friendship. Finny can come to this acceptance because he himself bears no guilt.

Gene, however, comes to bear a hideous sense of shame as a result of breaking the understood rules of the game, try as he may to suppress that fact. Initially, he manages to conceal from himself the implications of his act. He forgets that Leper had watched him push Finny, and he does not consciously assimilate the fact that Leper has withdrawn from him. Nor does he fully realize the extent to which his classmates blame and mistrust him, though he is certainly given a strong indication in the Butt Room. Not until Leper goes away, escaping from the military, and Gene visits him, does Gene realize Leper's resentment about his responsibility. Gene, however, strangely rationalizes his role in Finny's fall and begins to feel that he has in some way taken the place of Finny. He becomes the overreacher who tries to destroy his double and usurp his function. In terms of game theory, he has taken Finny out of the game and attempts to serve as a stand-in. He tries to play two roles simultaneously.

Consequently, it is hardly accidental that, after maiming Finny, Gene begins to wear his clothing, even his pink shirt. He remarks with satisfaction: "when I looked in the mirror it was no remote aristocrat I had become, no character out of daydreams. I was Phineas, Phineas to the life. I even had his humorous expression in my face, his sharp, optimistic awareness. I had no idea why this gave me such intense relief, but it seemed, standing there in Finny's triumphant shirt, that I would never stumble through the confusions of my own character again" (p. 51). Gene now thinks of himself as truly aristocratic and complete, as having altogether usurped the role of, and therefore destroyed, his opponent. Gene even affects the athletic aspirations of Finny, thinking, ". . . I lost part of myself to him then [when Finny says Gene has to play sports now that he cannot], and a soaring sense of freedom revealed that this must have been my purpose from the first: to become a part of Phineas" (p. 72). To their "joint double amazement," Gene shows promise as an athlete when trained by Finny. He even starts to resemble Finny's grimacing when irritated. And at Finny's funeral, Gene thinks of it as his own, admitting to himself that what Finny felt, knew and understood has somehow become what Gene now feels, knows and understands. A clutching, grasping player, he dominates and absorbs his friend, so that he can alone survive this game.

Finally, however, Gene puts things into better perspective. How long that takes is uncertain, but he has achieved that new perspective sometime between his graduation and his return to Devon fifteen years after the accident. During that time, his perception, the way in which he sees reality, especially himself, has undergone a great transition. By that time, he knows how complementary he and Finny were, and also how much his guilt has transmuted the full horror of his deed into something relatively worthwhile. Finny's fall from the tree has symbolically become Gene's fall from grace, his entry into the world of pain and suffering from which he can escape only by guilt and expiation. As a result of his breaking the rules of one game, another, more difficult game is introduced.

Initially, Gene refuses to accept all the implications of his deed. It is true that he tries to tell Finny of his guilt, but when Finny thinks of Gene as momentarily crazed, Gene does not dispute that position and suppresses his guilt. This guilt remains suppressed until the time of the kangaroo court when it is dredged up and finally confronted. Ironically, the motto over the building in which the trial takes place is the Latin inscription for "Here Boys Come to be Made Men" (p. 148). Here, too, another game begins, the trial itself in which Gene finds himself opposing the rest of the class. On this occasion Gene must finally surrender his pretenses and lies, placing himself fully within the confines of this new game, becoming honest with himself and Finny, so that Finny can finally accept Gene's private apology to him and his statement that he belongs with Finny, his veiled statement of love. When Gene can admit that there is something deadly in his love for everything, something for which he alone can be held responsible, then he can begin to profit morally and spiritually from his fall, his own *Felix Culpa*.

With that admission, the hell that he has been experiencing and the game that he has been playing—represented so aptly by the winter weather that "paralyzed the railroad yards"—and the unseemliness of the Butt Room and the kangaroo court, begin to abate. He comes to learn that "feeling becomes stronger than thought," that his relationship with Finny could have been based not upon rivalry but playfulness and instinctual love, and that the conflict between the opposing forces or doubles might have been resolved. As he says on coming back to Devon: "Everything at Devon slowly changed and slowly harmonized with what had gone before. So it was logical to hope that since the buildings and the Deans and the curriculum could achieve this, I could achieve, perhaps unknowingly already had achieved, this growth and harmony myself" (p. 4). At this time in Gene's life, he seems to have reconciled his past with the attributes that make up his personality—though the reader must still remember that Gene does say that for him life is still a war, agonistic conflict projected to a universal level.

What Gene must finally understand—and in this respect his knowledge is deeper and more profound than Finny's who for a long time locked out awareness of Gene's deceitfulness and guilt—is that the root of his hate, the root of the rivalry and competition so prevalent in Devon, and the root of the war which to him represents America, is in fact "something ignorant in the human heart" (p. 183). And that ignorance has nothing to do with the lack of knowledge or intelligence but with some intrinsically selfish quality that willfully destroys such games of peace and innocence as Finny and Devon contained in the summer of '42. With that understanding, Gene may be able to reach out to others in the way Finny did; he may be able to show love; he may be able to establish fidelity and trust; he may be able to play with honesty the games of human relationships; he may be able to work toward balance and harmony in order to bring the double aspects of the human being into alignment. But, as Jake Barnes qualifies of Brett's optimistic statement about the possibility of their love at the end of *The Sun Also Rises*: "Isn't it pretty to think so?"

Unfortunately, we do not see this new possibility put into practice after that fifteen-year hiatus between the end of school and Gene's return. Finny is dead, so the peace that Gene achieves will of necessity be a separate peace. He is apart from the conflict of the human heart, but, tragically, he cannot share that peace with the one whose death brought it into existence. And he may not be able to share that understanding with anyone else. Insofar as he recognizes Finny's worth and insofar as he takes the blame on his own shoulders, there is hope that the narrator of *A Separate Peace* has in fact achieved a lasting peace which he can share with others, a peace which replaces war-like competition and so brings *paidia* and *agon* together. The perception itself may be illumination enough to bring about the hoped for understanding and change.

Notes

3. "Levels of Meaning in *A Separate Peace*," *The English Record*, 18 (April 1968), 34–40.

4. Otto Rank, *The Double: A Psychoanalytic Study*, trans. and intro. Harry Tucker, Jr. (New York, 1971), pp. 69–86, and Ralph Tymms, *Doubles in Literary Psychology* (Cambridge, 1949), pp. 40–41.

5. Otto Rank, *Beyond Psychology* (New York, 1941; repr. 1958), p. 78, and C. F. Keppler, *The Literature of the Second Self* (Tucson, 1972), pp. 14–26.

9. Keppler, p. 11.

10. Keppler, p. 28.

11. Franziska Lynn Grailing, "The Theme of Freedom in *A Separate Peace*," *The English Journal*, 56 (Dec. 1967), 1269–72, finds that this use of Greek imagery is central to the book's notion of the individual's freedom to fulfill his own excellences.

12. Claire Rosenfield, "The Shadow Within: The Conscious and Unconscious Uses of the Double," in *Stories of the Double*, ed. Albert J. Guerard (Philadelphia, 1967), p. 326.

15. James Ellis discusses the motif of the fall in the book (pp. 313–18).

JAMES HOLT MCGAVRAN ON MALE BONDING IN THE NOVEL

What did Gene fear at Devon? Unlike Finny and most of the other students, he comes from a less elitist part of the country than New England (apparently West Virginia, Knowles's home state) but affects, with indifferent success, the speech and attitude of an aristocrat from "three states south of . . . [his] own" (148). At one point, when Gene says "I don't guess I did," Finny responds, "stop talking like a Georgia cracker" (112–13). But Gene is not socially disadvantaged at Devon by competition with blue-blood preppies from Boston or New York; not only is he the class brain and a more than passable athlete, but conservative student leader Brinker Hadley wants Gene to be his best friend—and so does emotionally disturbed Leper Lepellier. . . .

Foucault's emphasis on the policing of alternative sexualities had been taken up earlier in Eve Kosofsky Sedgwick's pathbreaking work on what she calls male homosocial desire.

Sedgwick's theorizing about men's relationships in patriarchal societies, recorded in *Between Men* (1985) and *Epistemology of the Closet* (1990), is based on the cultural paradox that while boys and men are expected to study, play, work, and fight together— both in competition and cooperation—they are absolutely forbidden to engage in sexual relations with each other. Thus the flip side of male homosocial bonding is homophobia, an irrational loathing of homosexuality, and what Sedgwick calls homosexual panic, the terrible fear that sets in whenever a man even unconsciously feels attracted to another male, feels the other may be attracted to him, or thinks that anyone else may suspect them of sexual feelings for each other (*Between Men* 1–5, 88–89). In other words, such traditional patriarchal societies as those of the white English-speaking world—and most certainly that of the elite boys' boarding school—almost set up boys and young men to fall in love with each other and yet threaten them with social ostracism and mental and physical abuse if they express their feelings openly. Sedgwick says tellingly, "For a man to be a man's man is separated only by an invisible, carefully blurred, always-already-crossed line from being 'interested in men'" (*Between Men* 89). . . .

I do not mean to imply by any of this that either Gene or Finny can be simply and reductively construed as gay; indeed labeling is only negatively related to what this gratifyingly deep book is about. I have a hunch, however, that had Finny lived longer, or had the Carnival mood not been interrupted by Leper's telegram, either boy might have seen the patriarchal proscription on homosexual activity as just another rule to be broken; one might have suggested such an experiment to the other; and the other might have accepted. But I do not suggest that we read *A Separate Peace* as even a failed coming-out story. While there are some hints, as I will show later, that Gene has had homosexual experience since Finny's death, Knowles leaves open the question of Gene's adult sexual orientation, I believe intentionally and partly for historical reasons. Knowles was recreating a World War II-era experience in the late 1950s, a decade before the Stonewall uprisings of 1969 commonly used to date the start of the late-twentieth-century gay liberation movement and a time when both the now-current vocabulary of liberation and the editorial will to publish such stories were lacking. But I hazard a guess that Knowles had a second reason for his silence regarding Gene's subsequent orientation: according to the current general understanding, "coming out" refers to a one-time, one-way move from the safe side of Sedgwick's always-already-crossed line to the other whereas, as Sedgwick herself and others argue, and as Knowles's text seems to support, gender roles and sexual identity are in reality far more fluid and contingent. Many young men and women experiment with same-sex intimacy, especially in adolescence, but later become committed partners in heterosexual relationships; and of course, for some the reverse can also be true. In what follows I will look first at some of Gene's and Finny's expressions of love for each other, then at Gene's growing sense of identification with Finny and Finny's reciprocating responses, and finally at three moments in the novel—their clandestine overnight trip to the beach, their last conversation before Finny's death, and Gene's final summation of his friendship—where the homoerotic tide seems to flow the highest.

As the time of the novel shifts to the past, Gene begins to remember Finny's physical presence, and he remembers this in great detail. First it is his voice: "'What I like best about this tree,' he said in that voice of his, the equivalent in sound of a hypnotist's eyes, 'what I like is that it's such a cinch!' He opened his green eyes wider and gave us his maniac look, and only the smirk on his wide mouth with its droll, slightly protruding upper lip reassured us that he wasn't completely goofy" (6). Then it is his athletic body: "We just looked quietly back at him, and so he began taking off his clothes, stripping down to his underpants. For such an extraordinary athlete . . . he was not spectacularly built. He was my height—five feet eight and a half inches. . . . He weighed a hundred and fifty pounds, a galling ten pounds more than I did, which flowed from his legs to torso around shoulders to arms and full strong neck in an uninterrupted, unemphatic unity of strength" (8). Gene comes back again and again, as the narrative progresses, to these or similar details of Finny's physical appearance. He realizes that Finny's beauty lies less in his actual shape or dimensions "he was not spectacularly built"—than in the way he inhabits his body, the energy that flows through him in a "unity of strength." This energy, which Gene later, at the Winter Carnival, calls Finny's "choreography of peace" (128), informs nearly everything Finny does: "He could also shine at many other things, with people for instance, the others in our dormitory, the faculty; in fact, if you stopped to think about it, Finny could shine with everyone, he attracted everyone he met. I was glad of that too. Naturally. He was my roommate and my best friend" (32). It seems Gene both is and is not jealous of his friend's attractiveness: there is pain as well as joy in that stand-alone "Naturally."

Later, during the period when he wrongly suspects Finny of wanting to subvert his studying and spoil his grades, he still burns with love for him, and years later, recalling this time when fear and joy clashed, the grown-up Gene cannot help writing a passionately poetic litany of love:

> Sometimes I found it hard to remember his treachery, sometimes I discovered myself thoughtlessly slipping back into affection for him again. It was hard to remember when one summer day after another broke with a cool effulgence over us, and there was a breath of widening life in the morning air—something hard to describe—an oxygen intoxicant, a shining northern paganism, some odor, some feeling so hopelessly promising that I would fall back in my bed on guard against it. It was hard to remember in the heady and sensual clarity of these mornings; I forgot whom I hated and who hated me. I wanted to break out crying from stabs of hopeless joy, or intolerable promise, or because these mornings were too full of beauty for me, because I knew of too much hate to be contained in a world like this. (47) . . .

Gene's love for Finny clearly is reciprocated. After their first jump from the tree into the river, when Leper and some other boys refuse to try it, "'It's you, pal,' Finny said to me at last, 'just you and me.' He and I started back across the fields, preceding the others like two seigneurs" (10). They wrestle with each other, partly for the fun of it, partly for the excitement of the physical contact, partly to be deliberately late for dinner. Finny always wins these skirmishes, until Gene sneak-attacks: "I threw my hip against his, catching him by surprise, and he was instantly down, definitely pleased. This was why he liked me so much. When I jumped on top of him, my knees on his chest, he couldn't ask for anything better. We struggled in some equality for a while, and then when we were sure we were too late for dinner, we broke off" (11). Caught by surprise? Finny's obvious delight at having Gene on top of him suggests that this was his goal all along. Much later, calling long distance from his home near Boston, Finny is relieved to hear that Gene has not chosen another roommate (75–76). Back at Devon, Finny watches with keen interest as Gene undresses after a grueling day of shoveling snow in a nearby railroad yard, criticizing all of his clothes but the stinking, sweaty undershirt next to his skin: "'There. You should have worn that all day, just that. That has real taste. The rest of your outfit was just gilding that lily of a sweat shirt'" (96). But Gene has a stronger (because not veiled in irony) proof of Finny's love the next morning, when Finny hears that Gene has told Brinker he will enlist and enter the war: "'Enlist!' cried Finny . . . His large and clear eyes turned with an odd expression on me. I had never seen such a look in them before. After looking at me closely he said, 'You're going to enlist?'" (99). Gene realizes the full significance of Finny's response and immediately gives up all thought of joining the war:

Phineas was shocked at the idea of my leaving. In some way he needed me. He needed me. I was the least trustworthy person he had ever met. I knew that; he knew or should know that too. I had even told him. But there was no mistaking the shield of remoteness in his face and voice. He wanted me around. The war then passed away from me, and dreams of enlistment and escape and a clean start lost their meaning for me. . . . I have never since forgotten the dazed look on Finny's face when he thought that on the first day of his return to Devon I was going to desert him. I didn't know why he had chosen me, why it was only to me that he could show the most humbling sides of his handicap. I didn't care. (100–101)

Gene no longer cares about the war, but Brinker does, and he will have his revenge at being jilted by Gene later, in the mock-trial that leads to Finny's death.

Gene's desire to become part of Finny, implicit in some of the passages already quoted, becomes explicit soon after Finny's fall, sometimes with clear homoerotic implications. Dressing for dinner one night, Gene has an odd but irresistible temptation to try on Finny's clothes, most notably his bright pink shirt: "But when I looked in the mirror it was no remote aristocrat I had become, no character out of daydreams. I was Phineas, Phineas to the life. I even had his humorous expression in my face, his sharp, optimistic awareness. . . . I would never stumble through the confusions of my own character again" (54). This identification gains in significance if we remember that earlier, when Finny first showed him the shirt, Gene had exclaimed, "Pink! It makes you look like a fairy!" and Finny had mildly replied, "I wonder what would happen if I looked like a fairy to everyone" (17).[1]

Later, when the crew manager Cliff Quackenbush calls Gene a "maimed son of a bitch" (71), Gene reacts immediately and violently: "I hit him hard across the face. I didn't know why for an instant; it was almost as though I were maimed. Then the realization that there was someone who was flashed over me" (71). Shortly thereafter, when Gene tells him on the telephone that he is "too busy for sports," Finny groans melodramatically for some time and finally says: "'Listen, pal, if I can't play sports, you're going to play them for me,' and I lost part of myself to him then, and a soaring sense of freedom revealed that this must have been my purpose from the first: to become a part of Phineas" (77). This is Gene's clearest, most explicit statement of his desire to merge permanently with his friend.

Gene later describes the rank air of the Devon gym in oddly nostalgic detail and ends with a surprisingly intimate comparison: "sweat predominated, but it was richly mingled with smells of paraffin and singed rubber, of soaked wool and liniment, and for those who could interpret it, of exhaustion, lost hope and triumph and bodies battling against each other. I thought it anything but a bad smell. It was preeminently the smell of the human body after it had been used to the limit, such a smell as has meaning and poignance for any athlete, just as it has for any lover" (105). Gene never speaks of his postwar, post-Finny personal life. That very silence, coupled with this association of male sweat and lovemaking, opens the possibility that he has at least experimented with homosexual activity because of the desire that Finny first awoke in him. But Knowles does not make this explicit, presumably for the reasons mentioned earlier.

After Gene accedes to Finny's demand to play sports for him, a number of things happen rather quickly. First, Gene replies "not exactly" when Finny says the gym is the "same same old place" (106). He further recalls: "He made no pretense of not understanding me. After a pause he said, 'You're going to be the big star now,' in an optimistic tone, and then added with some embarrassment, 'You can fill any gaps or anything'" (106). Then Finny does three things: he starts Gene doing chin-ups; he tells him his fantasy that there isn't any war; and when Gene quizzes him as to why he alone knows there is no war, Finny lays himself open to Gene in a way he never has before: "The momentum of the argument abruptly broke from his control. His face froze. 'Because I've suffered,' he burst out" (108). This is the beginning of Finny's training Gene to become a star athlete and Gene's tutoring Finny in his studies (111), and it leads to Gene's miraculous self-discovery when he gets a second wind and, though he does not say it, for a moment feels like Finny: "I lost myself, oppressed mind along with aching body; all entanglements were shed, I broke into the clear" (112). Shortly afterward, Gene comments: "He drew me increasingly away from . . . all other friends, into a world inhabited by just himself and me, where there was no war at all, just Phineas and me alone among all the other people in the world, training for the Olympics of 1944" (119). But before those never-to-be-held Olympics, Finny has another brain-child which he does bring off: the Winter Carnival. Although many arrangements are made, much hard cider is drunk, and several of their friends participate, there are two focal points of the carnival, and they involve Finny and Gene, respectively. The first is Finny's one-legged dance on top of the Prize Table: "Under the influence not I know of the hardest cider but of his own inner joy at life for a moment as it should be, as it was meant to be in his nature, Phineas recaptured that magic gift for existing primarily in space, one foot conceding briefly to gravity its rights before spinning him off again into the air. It was his wildest demonstration of himself, of himself in the kind of world he loved; it was his choreography of peace" (128). The second is Gene's weird, Finny-directed solo decathlon: "it wasn't cider which made me in this moment champion of everything he ordered, to run as though I were the abstraction of speed, to walk the half-circle of statues on my hands, to balance on my head on top of the icebox on top of the Prize Table . . . to accept at the end of it amid a clatter of applause . . . a wreath made from the evergreen trees which Phineas placed on my head" (128). By giving Gene all his athletic expertise, Finny gets back for a moment his own more-than-athletic grace and then happily sees Gene all but outdo him in goofiness, in "Finny-ness." The Jungian/Bakhtinian switching of identities could only be more complete if we knew that Finny started to make As on all his tests but sadly, there is not time for that to happen. The pent-up jealousies and suspicions of Brinker and Leper lead to the trial, with its Lenten atmosphere of accusation and doom, and thus to Finny's death.

A high point of their Edenic summer, shortly before Finny's wounding, is the forbidden bicycle trip to the beach that Finny proposes to Gene, perhaps the most overtly homoerotic sequence in the novel. Gene is aware that Finny "did everything he could think of for me" (39): he entertains Gene on the way by telling stories and jokes, doing bicycle gymnastics, and singing; after they get there and Gene gets tumbled in a wave, Finny plays in the surf for an hour, but all for Gene's amusement. Later, after eating hot dogs, they stroll along the beach and are keenly aware of each other's youthful beauty:

> Finny and I went along the Boardwalk in our sneakers and white slacks, Finny in a light blue polo shirt and I in a T-shirt. I noticed that people were looking fixedly at him, so I took a look myself to see why. His skin radiated a reddish copper glow of tan, his brown hair had been a little bleached by the sun, and I noticed that the tan made his eyes shine with a cool blue-green fire.
>
> "Everybody's staring at you," he suddenly said to me. "It's because of that movie-star tan you picked up this afternoon . . . showing off again." (39)

Gene's very next comment, spoken to himself after this declaration from Finny, sounds almost Sunday-schoolish: "Enough broken rules were enough that night" (39). Gene says this ostensibly with regard to drinking beer—each boy has only one glass—but it is also as if he knows he has had a proposition from Finny and is simply too frightened to accept. Then, before they go to sleep under the stars, Finny repeats his love song to Gene:

> The last words of Finny's usual nighttime monologue were, "I hope you're having a pretty good time here. I know I kind of dragged you away at the point of a gun, but after all you can't come to the shore with just anybody and you can't come by yourself, and at this teen-age period in life the proper person is your best pal." He hesitated and then added, "which is what you are," and there was silence on his dune. (40)

Again Gene isolates himself from the totally open intimacy Finny expresses, but this time he can't entirely refuse to understand it:

It was a courageous thing to say. Exposing a sincere emotion nakedly like that at the Devon School was the next thing to suicide. I should have told him then that he was my best friend also and rounded off what he had said. I started to; I nearly did. But something held me back. Perhaps I was stopped by that level of feeling, deeper than thought, which contains the truth. (40)

What can that deep, truthful level of feeling be but that the boys, far more than "best friends," are in love with each other? And what can stop the sexual expression of such love but what Sedgwick calls homosexual panic?

The same forces are at work in their last conversation before Finny dies. Both boys are crying as Finny finally confronts Gene's having made him fall out of the tree and Gene confronts their mutual love and desire:

"Then that was it. Something just seized you. It wasn't anything you really felt against me, it wasn't some kind of hate you've felt all along. It wasn't anything personal."

"No, I don't know how to show you, how can I show you, Finny? Tell me how to show you. It was just some ignorance inside me, some crazy thing inside me, something blind, that's all it was."

He was nodding his head, his jaw tightening and his eyes closed on the tears. "I believe you. It's okay because I understand and I believe you. You've already shown me and I believe you." (183)

Gene's agonized, desperate "Tell me how to show you" provides, in what turns out to be the last hours of Finny's life, his affirmative answer to Finny's naked emotions of love and desire expressed during their night on the beach. But now it is Finny's turn to demur; it is not clear whether his reply, "You've already shown me," should be read as a renewal of his own homosexual panic—here expressed in the magnanimous implication that their love is bigger than sex—or simply as an indicator of his extreme physical weakness.

Later that day he dies, leaving readers with many unanswered questions. If Finny had not thus absolved Gene before his death and Gene had not offered himself to Finny, could Gene have even gone on living for fifteen years, let alone return to Devon saying, as he does at the beginning of the novel (2), that he has finally escaped his boyhood fear?

But if Finny had lived and they had expressed their love physically, would even closer bonding have resulted, or would homophobia have reasserted itself in bitter division? Gene's comment on his grief, or rather the lack of it, strongly buttresses Butler's application of Freud's ideas on inner mourning to the repression of same-sex desire and the establishment of an outwardly heterosexual adult identity: "I did not cry then or ever about Finny. I did not cry even when I stood watching him being lowered into his family's strait-laced burial ground outside of Boston. I could not escape a feeling that this was my own funeral, and you do not cry in that case" (186). Of course these same words simultaneously confirm that Gene's union with Finny is complete and will always remain intact.

Trying to summarize Finny's continuing presence in his life at the end of the book, Gene writes a eulogy that underlines the fluidity and potential subversiveness of Finny's character—and thus, he seems to realize, of his own: "During the time I was with him, Phineas created an atmosphere in which I continued now to live, a way of sizing up the world with erratic and entirely personal reservations, letting its rocklike facts sift through and be accepted only a little at a time, only as much as he could assimilate without a sense of chaos and loss" (194). Still, Gene says that Phineas alone escaped the hostility of the world: "He possessed an extra vigor, a heightened confidence in himself, a serene capacity for affection which saved him" (194–95). The tone here and even the vocabulary are remarkably close to the benediction that Nick Carraway pronounces upon Jay Gatsby at the beginning of F. Scott Fitzgerald's famous novel of the 1920s: "If personality is an unbroken series of successful gestures, then there was something gorgeous about him, some heightened sensitivity to the promises of life, as if he were related to one of those intricate machines that register earthquakes ten thousand miles away" (Fitzgerald 2). Or compare the final words spoken by Henry, the narrator of David Guy's novel of adolescence *Second Brother*, about his best friend Sam, with whom he did share one homosexual experience: "My memory of Sam Golden is a talisman for me. I pick it up and hold it and it brings me luck. . . . When I think of how to live my life, not the things I want to do but the way I want to do them, I think of him. . . . I am glad I knew him. I am glad he lived" (Guy 264). Like Henry with Sam, like Nick with Gatsby, Gene is glad he knew Finny, glad he lived; there was something gorgeous about him. And, since Finny's "serene capacity for affection," coupled with his "choreography of peace" (128), now resides inside Gene, it saves him too, perhaps not from some continuing sense of loss, but from his feelings of guilt and fear.

Given the continuing strength of homophobia and homosexual panic in Western society, such a saving can still seem almost providential; but it has been almost half a century since Leslie Fiedler noted the paradox that our homophobic society somehow keeps a soft spot in its heart for texts like *The Adventures of Huckleberry Finn* that inscribe homoeroticism and compulsory heterosexuality side by side ("Come Back to the Raft Ag'in, Huck Honey!" 3–6). In another essay ("Wordsworth, Lost Boys, and Romantic Hom[e]ophobia") I have argued that some well-known and often-taught books for teenage boys let them down because the writers, probably affected by societal homophobia themselves, fail to explore same-sex relationships thoroughly and honestly. *A Separate Peace* is an exception: like *Huckleberry Finn*, Knowles's inscription of the love of Gene and Finny sets forth a brilliant and teachable example of the clash between the fluidity of gender and the restraints of homophobic discourse as it is played out on the adolescent male body.

Note

1. For the history of this shirt, first sold by Brooks Brothers in the early 1940s, see Bryant's "Phineas's Pink Shirt."

Works Cited

Berger, Maurice, Brian Wallis, and Simon Watson, eds. *Constructing Masculinity*. New York: Routledge, 1995.

Bristol, Michael D. "'Funeral Bak'd-Meats': Carnival and the Carnivalesque in Hamlet." In *Hamlet*, ed. Wofford, 348–67.

Bryant, Hallman Bell. "Phineas's Pink Shirt in John Knowles' *A Separate Peace*." *Notes on Contemporary Literature* 14 (1984): 5–6.

———. *"A Separate Peace": The War Within*. Boston: Twayne, 1990.

Butler, Judith. *Bodies That Matter: On the Discursive Limits of "Sex."* New York: Routledge, 1993.

———. *Gender Trouble: Feminism and the Subversion of Identity*. New York: Routledge, 1990.

———. "Melancholy Gender/Refused Identification." In *Constructing Masculinity*, ed. Berger, Wallis, and Watson, 21–36.

Devine, Joseph E. "The Truth about *A Separate Peace*." *English Journal* 58 (1969): 519–20; rpt. in *Readings*, ed. Karson, 122–24.

Fiedler, Leslie. "Come Back to the Raft Ag'in, Huck Honey!" In *A Fiedler Reader*. New York: Stein and Day, 1977. 3–12.

Fitzgerald, F. Scott. *The Great Gatsby*. New York: Scribner, 1925.

Foucault, Michel. *The History of Sexuality; An Introduction*, vol. 1. Trans. Robert Hurley. New York: Vintage, 1990.

Guy, David. *Second Brother*. New York: New American Library, 1985.

Karson, Jill, ed. *Readings an A Separate Peace*, San Diego: Greenhaven, 1999.

Knowles, John. *A Separate Peace*. New York: Bantam, 1966.

McGavran, James Holt. "Wordsworth, Lost Boys, and Romantic Hom[e]ophobia." In *Literature and the Child: Romantic Continuations, Postmodern Contestations*, ed. James Holt McGavran. Iowa City: University of Iowa Press, 1999. 130–52.

Mengeling, Marvin E. "*A Separate Peace*: Meaning and Myth." *English Journal* 58 (1969): 1322–29.

Sarotte, Georges-Michel. *Like a Brother, Like a Lover: Male Homosexuality in the American Novel and Theater from Herman Melville to James Baldwin*. Garden City: Doubleday Anchor, 1978.

Sedgwick, Eve Kosofsky. *Between Men: English Literature and Male Homosocial Desire*. New York: Columbia University Press, 1985.

———. *Epistemology of the Closet*. Berkeley: University of California Press, 1990.

Slethaug, Gordon E. "The Play of the Double in *A Separate Peace*." *Canadian Review of American Studies* 15 (1984): 259–70.

Witherington, Paul. "*A Separate Peace*: A Study in Structural Ambiguity." *English Journal* 54 (1965), 795–800; rpt. in *Readings*, ed. Karson, 79–88.

Wofford, Susanne L., ed. *Hamlet*. Boston: Bedford/St. Martin's, 1994.

A third level of meaning in the novel concerns sin and forgiveness. The outward form of the sin is Gene's betrayal of Finny by making him fall from the tree. The real meaning of this sinful act, as is true of all sinful acts, is separation. As we are told the details of the almost ideal friendship between Gene and Finny in the first part of the novel, we gradually see that Gene and Finny are almost one person. They are the same height and almost the same weight, they are roommates, they wear each other's clothes, they collaborate instinctively in breaking the rules of Devon School, they say their silent prayers together before going to sleep, they are the only boys daring enough to jump from the tree, and they do this together. One excels in mind; the other in body. Gene breaks this nearly perfect unity when he resents Finny's persuasive leadership, and he makes the gulf greater when he gives in to the ugly suspicion that Finny is trying to destroy his scholastic record. This separation is the state of sin that the novel explores. It leads to Finny's fall from the tree, which, as a spiritual fall, is just as serious a fall for Gene, his *alter ego*. Finny is physically crippled afterwards. Gene is spiritually crippled, or maimed, to use the word John Knowles uses in the Quackenbush incident a little later in the novel.

Knowles does not stop with giving us an understanding of the essence of sin. Through the remarkable character of Finny we also gain an understanding of the desired sequel to sin— forgiveness. When Gene visits Finny, now an invalid, in his Boston home before the fall session begins and tells him that he deliberately jounced him off the limb, Finny flatly rejects the idea. Later in the fall term when Finny comes back late to school, he is delighted to be Gene's roommate again. When he hears that Gene might enlist in the armed forces, he is shocked and depressed. Seeing this reaction, Gene in amazement thinks to himself, "He needed me. I was the least trustworthy person he had ever met. I knew that; he knew or should know that too. I had even told him. I had told him. But there was no mistaking the shield of remoteness in his face and voice. He wanted me around." (p. 132)

This reconciliation leads to an even closer unity of Gene and Finny than before the fall. Finny is filled with joy when Gene drops his plans to enlist. The two experience again for a while the special peace they had enjoyed during the summer session. With Gene tutoring Finny in studies and Finny tutoring Gene in sports, Gene accomplishes amazing physical feats, and Finny almost becomes a good student. Their harmony, however, is suddenly shattered when their friend, Brinker Hadley, forces them to attend a mock investigation into Finny's accident, at which Gene's guilt is brought to light. Finny cannot reject the truth this time, and rushing out of the room in a rage with his leg still in a cast, he falls down a marble stairway and breaks his leg again. But in the hospital the next day he finds the power in himself to overcome hatred and forgive Gene. This forgiveness purifies Gene's spirit so that when the time comes he can enter the war undefiled: "I had no qualms at all; in fact I could feel now the gathering, glowing sense of sureness in the face of it. I was ready for the war, now that I no longer had any hatred to contribute to it. My fury was gone, I felt it gone, dried up at the source, withered and lifeless. Phineas had absorbed it and taken it with him, and I was rid of it forever." (p. 255.) Christ-like, with his body broken for Gene, Finny loves, forgives, and helps to make whole the man who has betrayed him. E. M. Forster has said that *A Separate Peace* reminds him of the *Philoctetes* of Sophocles. Perhaps he saw in this situation a parallel between Finny with his crippled leg and Philoctetes with his wounded leg, both of whom forgave and saved their betrayers.

Another level of meaning in the novel is the way it considers the predicament of a good man in a corrupt world. This timeless theme is seen in much of the world's great literature: the story of Joseph, Job, Christ, Hamlet, Tolstoy's "Ivan the Fool," Dostoevsky's *The Idiot*, and Ibsen's *An Enemy of the People*. Phineas of *A Separate Peace* is a brother to the central characters in these stories. He has the winning charm and nobility of spirit of these other heroes. Like them he is at variance with the corrupt world around him. During the idyllic summer session at Devon in 1942 while the rest of the world is engaged in an inhuman conflict, Finny is the leader of a small band of sixteen-year-olds who find a separate peace. When Gene remembers how perfect that summer was, he pictures Finny balanced joyfully on one foot on the front of a canoe going down the river, looking as though he were a god about to take off into the air, the embodiment of summer, youth, innocence, and goodness. After he is crippled and cannot hope to take part in World War II, Finny half playfully pretends and makes Gene pretend that the war is a fake, that it is all a charade created by corrupt, fat old men in order to prevent young people from taking away their power and luxuries. To Finny the rest of the world is a madhouse, a "Funny Farm." (p. 143.)

The world usually will not tolerate a good man who sees through its corruption. It usually breaks and destroys the good man as it did Christ, Hamlet, and Prince Myshkin. It breaks Finny physically and almost breaks him spiritually, but after giving in temporarily to hate, he quickly regains his integrity. The world destroys his body, but not his spirit.

Probing the novel further for other levels of meaning, we find it is also a novel about war and peace. The war is the macrocosm of *A Separate Peace*. It is out there, remote from the mercifully, although temporarily, spared sixteen-year-olds in the blissful summer session at Devon. Finny and his small band of pals make up the microcosm. These boys at this time are too young for military training. The adult world looks on them with fond wistfulness, spoiling them a bit, allowing them to break a few rules, because the adults know that in a year or so these boys may be dying at the battlefronts. There seems to be an unspoken agreement to allow this age group to have a last fling at peace. Peace takes the form of frequent unscheduled swims in the river, missing meals to stay out and play longer, cutting classes, an illegal bike trip to the seashore for swimming and sleeping all night on the beach, making up an imaginative athletic game and playing it every day, and setting a new speed record in the school's swimming pool just for the fun of it and telling no one. After Finny's accident this special kind of peace disappears for a while, but then when Finny returns to school, peace comes back again, this time in the form of training Gene for the never-to-be-held 1944 Olympic Games and in the form of the glorious, wild Winter Carnival organized by Finny. The peace of this microcosm is epitomized by Finny dancing "his choreography of peace" (p. 169.) on one leg (the other still in a cast) on the prize table.

The war, however, cannot be kept from encroaching occasionally on this island of peace. Food and luxury shortages increase. Large numbers of Devon boys are recruited to save the local apple crop and to shovel the Boston railroad yards out from under a paralyzing snowfall. But Gene and Finny do not feel the horror of the war until the first boy from Devon to enlist, Leper Lepellier, cracks up mentally during his basic training. The grim reality of Leper's failure makes Finny give up his playful fantasy that the war is a hoax. By contrasting the Devon idyll with the evil war of the outside world, Knowles lets us see that there is more sense in Finny's nonsense world of peace than in the real world of war.

The deepest and most important level of meaning in *A Separate Peace* is the struggle for self-knowledge and maturity. To understand this meaning we must recognize that Gene, not Finny, is the central character of the book, just as the young sea captain, not Leggatt, is the central character of Conrad's *The Secret Sharer* and Marlow, not Kurtz, is the central character of *The Heart of Darkness*. As in these two Conrad works, which *A Separate Peace* resembles in theme and purpose, the narrating central character (Gene) identifies himself with another character (Finny) who occupies most of his thoughts. Eventually in all three of these novels the narrator finds himself through his identification with the other person. Finny is such an admirable character and he is talked about so much that there is a natural temptation to consider him the protagonist, but we should see that the main struggle in the novel is Gene's.

Even when we first meet Finny, he knows who he is and has a healthy way of facing life; he possesses unusual self-confidence and wholeness for a boy so young. It is not surprising that Gene and the other boys naturally look to him as their leader. It is Gene who is lacking in wholeness. We see this in his fear of jumping from the tree even though he is quite capable of doing it successfully. We see it in his growing resentment of Finny's power over him. We see it in his mistaken notion that Finny is trying to hurt his academic record. We see it most of all when Gene shakes Finny from the tree even after he knew that his suspicions of Finny were unjust. This cruel act in the tree, however, marks the beginning of Gene's self-discovery. He courageously forces himself to see the savage darkness in his heart that caused him to turn against Finny, and he manfully confesses to Finny. Finny's rejection of the confession prevents Gene's immediate recovery. Gene must return to school in the fall spiritually maimed. His refusal to go out for sports is a sign of this. When Finny calls Gene up long distance from his home and offers his healing forgiveness, Gene's spirit begins to lose its sickness: ". . . I lost part of myself to him then, and a soaring sense of freedom revealed that this must have been my purpose from the first: to become a part of Phineas." (p. 103.) In losing himself to Finny he began to find himself.

Gene does not achieve self-knowledge and maturity, however, until after two more painful incidents in the novel, Leper's breakdown and Finny's rebreaking of his leg. When Gene visits Leper in his Vermont home after Leper's crack-up and "escape" from the army, Leper with the unerring insight that his own illness gives him accuses Gene of always being "a savage underneath" (p. 180.) and cites his knocking Finny out of the tree as evidence. Gene has to face this ugly truth again as well as the possibility that he might lose his sanity in the war just as Leper did. After the second breaking of Finny's leg Gene must relive his guilt, and Finny cannot reject the truth that was so clearly brought out at the mock investigation. In the hospital room both Gene and Finny face the truth about Gene, and about all mankind, the truth that there is a blind, ignorant, crazy evil in the heart of man.

After the agony of these experiences of self-realization, Gene can accept the death of Finny with manly sorrow but no weak tears, and he can enter the war without false heroism and without hating the enemy. He now understands the cause of war. He will not be driven out of his senses by the incomprehensibility of it as Leper was, and he will not childishly blame it on the older generation as Brinker does. Gene sees now "that wars were made instead by something ignorant in the human heart." (p. 252.) He tells us that he has already killed his enemy. His enemy is his youthful innocence, personified by Finny; his enemy is his former ignorance of the darkness that lurks in his heart and in the hearts of all men. . . .

Another level of meaning previously examined, the understanding of sin and forgiveness, is also thoroughly intertwined with the primary theme of self-knowledge. Gene sins because he does not know himself or his *alter ego* Finny well enough. Finny's forgiveness of Gene cures Gene of his separation from Finny and from himself. The idea that Finny is a modern illustration of the good man in a corrupt world is closely tied in with the struggle for self-knowledge too. Although he is Finny's best friend, Gene represents, even better than the fat old men that Finny ridicules, the corruption of the world that destroys Finny. The essence of the world's corruption is that universal savagery of which a part is found in Gene's soul. Gene's discovery of this evil in himself while in the tree takes place at the same time as his betrayal of his friend and leads to the loss of Finny. The cost of self-discovery in a world as corrupt as ours is usually high. In this case the cost is the destruction of the one supremely good man Gene knows.

Finally, the novel's treatment of the conflict between war and peace further supports the theme of self-knowledge. Another part of Gene's gradual understanding of himself is his ridding himself of fear of the war. This vague fear of the war was part of his immaturity; it is another word for the enemy that he says he killed while still at school. In the conclusion of the novel Gene tells us how various other people tried to cope with the thought of war. Some tried to pretend that they were humble ants not worthy to be involved in such a gigantic menace. Some, like Mr. Ludsbury, tried, by asserting their superiority to the whole mess, to remain aloof from it. People like Quackenbush tried to fight it with practical schemes to avoid combat duty. Brinker and others like him took refuge in resentment against the older generation that supposedly caused the war. Others like Leper met the horror face to face and lost their minds. Only Finny knew how to regard the war or any other evil; his way was with confidence in himself, with no fear or hatred of anyone else, and with a sense that occasional bursts of animosity are part of everyone's human nature. Through his life and character he imparted this wisdom to Gene, and in this way Gene found himself and became a man.

H.B. Bryant on Phineas's Pink Shirt

In American literature there are at least three works where pink items of apparel figure importantly. The first is the pink ribbon worn by Faith in Hawthorne's short story "Young Goodman Brown," the second is Gatsby's pink suit in Fitzgerald's *The Great Gatsby*, and the third is the pink shirt worn by Phineas, the main character in John Knowles' novel *A Separate Peace*. The significance of the first two items has been commented upon extensively but the latter has received no more than passing notice by critics of Knowles' novel.

Phineas's pink shirt is an object of considerable importance both as a symbol of the protagonist's personality and as a means to enhance the historical ambience Knowles creates in the early pages of the novel. The plot events of *A Separate Peace* took place over a period of two years, starting with the summer session of 1942 and ending with the 1943 Commencement at the Devon School. The novel centers on the relationship of two boys, Gene Forrester and Phineas, nicknamed "Finny," who are roommates at a New England prep school during the first years of World War Two.

This era is evoked vividly by Knowles in a number of ways. He alludes to popular songs of the day such as "Don't Sit Under the Apple Tree" and "They're Either Too Young or Too Old," and with references to America Tobacco Company's cigarette ads which patriotically claimed that "Lucky Strike Green has gone to war!" (meaning that the manufacturer has sacrificed the green shade that characterized the package and gone to a plain white pack so that the G.I.'s would have the use of the dye for olive drab).[1] Knowles, in fact, makes a point about this color. The prevailing color of life in America at that time, he writes, is "a dull green called olive. That color is always respectable and always important. Most others risk being unpatriotic."[2]

But it is the color pink rather than olive drab which I want to discuss. Finny's pink shirt is also a part of the period furniture which makes the enveloping action so authentic. If one looks back at fashion in men's clothing, it is surprising to find that colored dress shirts were once regarded as a radical fashion; in fact, America was divided into two classes by collar color: blue or white. Paradoxically, it was the conservative sartorial establishment of Brooks Brothers which introduced the pink shirt in the early 1940's to the staid world of male fashions. The pink button-down collar polo shirt was a historical garment—it was the first men's shirt ever in pink, and it caused such a stir that *Vogue* ran a picture of the shirt on the cover of the magazine.[3] Of course, the pink shirt has since become the badge of all so-called "preppies" and is worn by males and females alike. In 1942, however, it was novel enough to have quite a shock effect. While Finny's shirt is not identified by brand in the novel, it has the characteristics of the Brooks model; it is made of "a finely woven broad cloth that is carefully cut and very pink," with a high collar, and has a yoke-neck which Finny notes with approval; he says to Gene, "Did you ever see stuff like this, and a color like this? It does not even button all the way down. You have to pull it over your head. . ." (p. 17).

The unique features of the shirt are noticed by the conservative Gene, who asks Finny when he takes his proud possession (which his mother had bought for him) out of the drawer, "What's that thing?" He adds sarcastically that a pink shirt "makes you look like a fairy," but Finny is undaunted by such taunts. He does not seem troubled in the least by the imputation of effeminacy, replying to his roommate that his purpose in wearing the shirt is to make a statement about recent news of allied war victories. He claims that he has donned the shirt "as an emblem," which he will wear in lieu of a flag since they "can't float Old Glory proudly out of the window" (p. 18).

Finny does indeed wear his pink shirt proudly; "Something no one else in the school could have done without some risk of having it torn from his back," Gene remarks. The shirt becomes like a talisman for Finny. During the course of the day he wears it to his classes; disarming the critical queries of teachers who ask about his oddly colored shirt, and amusing even the sternest headmaster, Mr. Patch-Withers, with his explanation for the shocking pink shirt.

This episode shows several things about the character of both Finny and Gene as well as the historical "character" of the period. In 1942 America and her allies had very little to cheer about. Most of our navy had been sunk at Pearl Harbor and our army defeated at Bataan and forced to undergo the horrors of the "Death March." Thus, a patriotic and exuberant teenager like Finny would have felt the need to celebrate an allied success, even a small one like a bombing raid on Central Europe. However, an extravagant gesture like wearing a shirt of such fancy cut and dainty color would be bound to draw derisive remarks in an all-male bastion like Devon School where suspicion of one's masculinity was something to guard against. It is a testament to Finny's self-confidence that he is willing to risk being called "a fairy." He, unlike his roommate Gene, knows who he is and he is not afraid of what others think.

This episode, as well as showing Finny's whimsical patriotism, his audacity, and inner assurance, by contrast shows Gene's limitations. He would never go against convention nor risk his image by doing something so bizarre as Finny does here. Gene is the type who follows "the rules," and the rules at this time and place did not yet allow one to wear a pink shirt with impunity, with the exception of Finny.

Notes

1. Richard R. Lingeman, *Don't You Know There's A War On?* (G. P. Putnam: New York, 1970), 1.

2. John Knowles, *A Separate Peace* (Bantam Editions, New York, 1972), p. 33; all citations are to this edition.

3. John Berendt, "Classics: The Button-Down Shirt," *Esquire* (April 1983), 32–34.

DAVID G. HOLBORN ON THE ROLE OF WAR IN THE NOVEL

The novel is set at Devon, a small New England prep school, during the Second World War. The details and atmosphere of such a school are realistically rendered in the dormitories and playing fields, the lawn parties and the truancies. Accuracy of fact and mood makes this an interesting and gripping story. But it is more than just a good story because it has at least two other dimensions. From beginning to end little Devon is impinged upon by the world at war, so much so that the ordinary round of prep school activities takes on a militaristic flavoring. Along with the outward pressures exerted by the war are the internal pressures, particularly in the narrator Gene, which lead to self-discovery and an acceptance of human ideals and human frailties. It is the integration of these three focuses that makes this such an effective and satisfying novel.

The novel opens with the narrator's return to Devon fifteen years after the action of the story he is about to tell. He presents two realistic scenes that later become associated with important events in the story: the First Academy Building, with its unusually hard marble floors that cause the second break in Phineas's leg; and the tree, that real and symbolic tree which is the place of Finny's initial accident and the presentation of lost innocence. These detailed places occasion the narrator's meditation, and suddenly through flashback we are transported to the idyllic summer of 1942. This framework narrative and flashback technique is important because it sets up a vehicle for conveying judgments to the reader about character and action from two perspectives: sometimes we are getting Gene's reaction at the moment and other times we are receiving the retrospective judgment of the mature man.

I mention this narrative technique not merely as a matter of literary style but as an indication of the serious, thoughtful quality of the novel. The author wishes us to see the growth of Gene and at the same time experience an exciting story, not a philosophical or psychological tract. This is deftly accomplished by means of the dual perspective. The following comment on the important motif of fear illustrates the mature man reflecting on the entire experience at Devon:

> Preserved along with it, like stale air in an unopened room, was the well-known fear which had surrounded and filled those days, so much of it that I hadn't even known it was there. Because, unfamiliar with the absence of fear and what that was like, I had not been able to identify its presence.
>
> Looking back now across fifteen years, I could see with great clarity the fear I had lived in, which must mean that in the interval I had succeeded in a very important undertaking: I must have made my escape from it. (2)

This statement is more philosophical and judgmental than most later reflective statements, since at this point the story proper has not even begun. But the mature man is heard at intervals throughout the novel, as in this analogy of war to a wave:

> So the war swept over like a wave at the seashore, gathering power and size as it bore on us. . . . I did not stop to think that one wave is inevitably followed by another even larger and more powerful, when the tide is coming in. (101)

Comments such as these encourage the reader to pause in the story and reflect on the significance of events, certainly an important thing to do with any novel but particularly with a novel of maturation.

The story proper begins in the summer of 1942. It is the calm before the storm, the storm of course being the world at war. For these boys—primarily Gene, Finny, and Leper—the war is still a year away. Even the faculty at Devon treat the reduced summer school class with a bemused tolerance. This summertime Devon is like Eden: the sun always seems to shine, the days endlessly filled with games on the playing fields. This Eden also has its tree and, like the original, this is the tree of the knowledge of good and evil. At first, however, it is just a tree, something to jump from into the clear cool waters of the Devon River. As idyllic as this summer and this particular game of jumping from the tree are, hints of the impending war keep creeping in. Jumping from the tree becomes a test of courage, a kind of boot camp obstacle. So, taking a cue from war literature, the boys call their jumping group the Super Suicide Society of the Summer Session. Always the consummate athlete, Finny jumps first with fluid grace and without apparent fear. Gene is reluctant, but cannot refuse the challenge. The two close buddies cement their friendship in this test. Leper, at least on this first occasion, does not jump. This foreshadows his later inability to cope with the pressures of the war. Already the superficial harmony of the summer is disrupted by this competition which separates the boys according to those who possess the particular skills and temperament necessary in the world of war and those who don't. The scene is a preparation for the key event of the book where Finny breaks his leg, and an early reminder that Eden cannot really exist in this world. . . .

Gene and Finny have a special relationship but it is not immune—at least on Gene's part—from the petty jealousies that infect most relationships. In Gene's own words, Finny is "too good to be true." He plays games, like the blitzball he invented, for the sheer joy of exhibiting his remarkable athletic skills. He is a natural. One day he breaks the school swimming record in the hundred yard freestyle, with Gene as the only witness, but has no desire to repeat it in an official meet. The idea of having done it is enough. And because of his affability, he can talk his way out of almost any jam, as he did the day he was caught at the headmasters lawn party wearing the school tie for a belt. One side of Gene admires Finny for these feats, while another, darker side envies him for his ability to glide through life unscathed. As Gene says about Finny after the party at the headmaster's:

> He had gotten away with everything. I felt a sudden stab of disappointment. That was because I just wanted to see some more excitement; that must have been it. (21)

The last statement is a rationalization, and a weak one at that. Knowles lets the rationalization stand without a direct statement of truth from the older man's perspective, but the irony leaves no doubt as to Gene's true feelings. Surely any reader, and particularly the youthful one, can identify with this ambivalent reaction to a friend's success. In the end Gene comes to understand and accept these feelings, and the book as a whole makes the statement that only by becoming conscious of these feelings, and coming to terms with them, can a person grow toward maturity. Refusing to face up to jealousies leads only to tragedies such as the one that occurs in this book.

Gene's envy of Finny comes to a head when he concludes wrongly that Finny is keeping him occupied with games so that his grades will suffer. Gene is the best student in the class and Finny the best athlete, but Gene thinks Finny wants him to jeopardize his supremacy in academics so Finny can shine more brightly. It is at this juncture in the book that the boys go off to the tree for what turns out to be the last meeting of the Super Suicide Society of the Summer Session.

The basic facts concerning Finny's fall from the tree that results in his broken leg are revealed in the first narration of the event, but the reader has to wait for the corroborating evidence presented by Leper months later at a mock trial, along with his peculiar emotional and artistic perception of the event. The facts as presented by Gene are that his knees bent and he "jounced the limb." It is impossible to know how much, if any, forethought was involved in the disastrous movement itself. What is clear from the juxtaposition of this event and the commentary that precedes it is that Gene reacts in some recess of his being, not, as we might have expected, to get back at Finny for hampering him in his studies, but out of a sudden awareness that Finny was not jealous of him, was not competing. It goes back to the statement that Finny is too good to be true. This is a particularly keen insight into the human heart; namely, that we often strike out at others not because of the harm they have done us but because their goodness sheds light on our own mistrustfulness.

In the case of Finny, his goodness is of a peculiar kind. He is not good from the faculty's point of view since he does not study very hard and breaks as many of the rules as he can. His is a kind of natural goodness, a harmoniousness with the sun, the earth and its seasons, and his fellow man—so long as his fellow man preserves his imagination and participates in Finny's rituals of celebration. It has justly been said that Finny is not a realistic character, yet he is an interesting one, and something more than a foil for Gene. Most readers have probably had childhood friends with some of the characteristics of Finny; it is in the sum of his parts that he deviates from reality.

Finny is a character fated to die, not because of anything he does, or anything anyone does to him—though Gene's action against him is significant—but because of what he is and what the world is. If the idyllic summer could have lasted forever, then Finny could have lived a full life. If winter Olympic games could have taken the place of fighting troops on skis, then Finny's leg might have been made whole again. But the world is at war and the first casualties—Leper and Finny—are those whose beings are antithetical to the disruption that is war. Finny's harmoniousness cannot coexist with the dislocation of war. Gene humorously acknowledges this when he says:

> "They'd get you some place at the front and there'd be a lull in the fighting, and the next thing anyone knew you'd be over with the Germans or the Japs, asking if they'd like to field a baseball team against our side. You'd be sitting in one of their command posts, teaching them English. Yes, you'd get confused and borrow one of their uniforms, and you'd lend them one of yours. Sure, that's what would happen. You'd get things so scrambled up nobody would

know who to fight anymore. You'd make a mess, a terrible mess, Finny, out of the war." (182)

To Finny, the war was like blitzball, a free-flowing, individualistic game, with no allies and no enemies. To Gene, though he doesn't like to admit it, the war was all too real before he even got to it, so much so that his best friend became his enemy.

Leper, the character third in importance in the book, is the one most directly affected by the war and the one whose testimony at the mock trial seals the truth of the tree incident. Leper returns to Devon after having a nervous breakdown in boot camp. He is the most sensitive of all the boys, a loner and a lover of nature. His testimony not only confirms what actually happened in the tree, but also, through descriptive imagery, places the event in the context of the war. Leper's distracted mind remembers all the concrete details of the scene. Finny and Gene were in the tree and Leper was looking up, with the sun in his eyes, "and the rays of the sun were shooting past them, millions of rays shooting past them like—like golden machine-gun fire." And when the two in the tree moved, "they moved like an engine." "The one holding on to the trunk sank for a second, up and down like a piston, and then the other one sank and fell" (166–168). Leper, who previously saw the world in terms of snails and beaver dams, sees the action in the tree in terms of engines and machine-guns. This is because of what the war has done to him, and more subtly, it is a commentary on how a game in a tree has become a wartime battle. All three boys are pummelled by the machine of war, because, as the book seems to tell us, war is a condition of the human heart and soul. . . .

But as much as this is a book about war—within and without—it is also a book about peace. The human heart stripped naked to reveal its pride and jealousy, is a cause for sober reflection. But the title, *A Separate Peace*, encourages the reader to pass with Gene through the sufferings of war to achieve a peace. This peace is based upon understanding and the growth that follows such understanding. Finny achieves one kind of separate peace, the peace of death; it is left to Gene to achieve a separate peace that will allow him to live with himself and others in the adult world, chastened and strengthened by his mistake. His words at the end show us that he has succeeded:

> I never killed anybody and I never developed an intense level of hatred for the enemy. Because my war ended before I ever put on a uniform; I was on active duty all my time at school; I killed my enemy there. (196)

This growth in awareness that leads Gene to his separate peace makes the ending of this book an optimistic one. Some readers seem to feel this book is another *Lord of the Flies*, a novel that depicts human nature when stripped of social institutions as reverting to a frighteningly depraved state. This is not the case in *A Separate Peace*. Once recognized and accepted the war within is tamed.

Furthermore, Knowles does not describe the weakness within as evil, but rather as a form of ignorance. After the mock trial, Gene tries to tell Finny what it was that caused him to jounce the limb: "It was just some ignorance inside me, some crazy thing inside me, something blind, that's all it was" (183). One chapter later war is described in the same terms by the narrator: "Because it seemed clear that wars were not made by generations and their special stupidities, but that wars were made by something ignorant in the human heart" (193). Most ignorance is not invincible; Gene proves this.

Work Cited
Knowles, John. *A Separate Peace*. 1960. New York: Bantam, 1966.

Works by John Knowles

A Separate Peace, 1959

Morning in Antibes, 1962

Double Vision; American Thoughts Abroad, 1964

Indian Summer, 1966

Phineas: Six Stories, 1968

The Paragon, 1971

Spreading Fires, 1974

A Vein of Riches, 1978

Peace Breaks Out, 1981

A Stolen Past, 1983

The Private Life of Axie Reed, 1986

Annotated Bibliography

Bryant, Hallman B. "Symbolic Names in Knowles's *A Separate Peace.*" *Names*, vol. 34 (March 1986): pp. 83–88.

Analyzes the significance and symbolism of the names of the two central characters. Hallman explains the roles of Gene and Finny and how they function in the novel, in relation to their names.

Bryant, Hallman B. *Understanding A Separate Peace: A Student Casebook to Issues, Sources, and Historical Documents.* Westport, Conn: Greenwood Press, 2002.

This study guide includes historical background of World War II and prep boarding schools, to help students see the connections between the fictional world of the novel and the real world during the years 1942–1945. Also includes a literary analysis of *A Separate Peace*, and commentary by Knowles.

Devine, Joseph. "The Truth About *A Separate Peace*," *The English Journal*, vol. 58, no. 4 (April 1969): pp. 519–520.

Instead of viewing Finny as a character of beauty, goodness, and innocence, Devine takes a contradictory critical stance. He argues that Finny is the villain and representative of the Nazis.

Ely, Sister M. Amanda. "The Adult Image in Three Novels of Adolescent Life," *The English Journal*, vol. 56, no. 8 (November 1967): pp. 1127–31.

Ely focuses on the adults in the novel. She argues they are out of touch and inadequate; the boys lack adult role models.

Halio, Jay L. "John Knowles's Short Novels." *Studies in Short Fiction*, vols. 1 and 2 (Winter 1964): pp. 107–112.

Halio focuses on the theme of fear in the novel and argues that Gene's violent act against Finny rises from that fear.

Greiling, Franziska Lynne. "The Theme of Freedom in *A Separate Peace*," *English Journal*, vol 56, no. 9 (December 1967): pp. 1269–72.

Compares *A Separate Peace* to Greek ideas, such as love of freedom and respect for the individual. The essay shows how Gene redeems himself and frees himself from jealousy and despair.

Kennedy, Ian. "Duel Perspective Narrative and the Character of Phineas in *A Separate Peace*." *Studies in Short Fiction*, vol. 11, no. 1 (Fall 1974): pp. 353–359.

Focuses on Knowles's narrative techniques, in showing Gene as a boy and as a man. By employing this method, Knowles overcomes the limitations of first-person narration.

Nora, Sister M. "A Comparison of Actual and Symbolic Landscape in *A Separate Peace*," *Discourse*, vol. 11, 1968, pp. 356–362.

Focuses on the Devon School setting, and how this is similar to the Phillips Exeter Academy, the school that Knowles attended.

Tribunella, Eric L. "Refusing the Queer Potential: John Knowles's *A Separate Peace*." *Children's Literature*, vol. 30. (2002): pp. 81–95.

A Separate Peace has been a source of controversy for possible underlying themes of homosexuality, but Tribunella argues that it is actually a tract for heterosexist development. Tribunella examines instances of homophobia, with Gene's violent act of pushing Finny from the tree symbolizing "homosexual panic."

Umphlett, Wiley Lee. "The New-Romantic Encounter." *The Sporting Myth and the American Experience*. Lewisburg, PA: Bucknell University Press, 1975.

Umphlett focuses on the character development of Phineas, suggesting that he is a specific type of hero: the dying athlete on a quest for immortality.

Contributors

Harold Bloom is Sterling Professor of the Humanities at Yale University. He is the author of 30 books, including *Shelley's Mythmaking, The Visionary Company, Blake's Apocalypse, Yeats, A Map of Misreading, Kabbalah and Criticism, Agon: Toward a Theory of Revisionism, The American Religion, The Western Canon,* and *Omens of Millennium: The Gnosis of Angels, Dreams, and Resurrection. The Anxiety of Influence* sets forth Professor Bloom's provocative theory of the literary relationships between the great writers and their predecessors. His most recent books include *Shakespeare: The Invention of the Human,* a 1998 National Book Award finalist, *How to Read and Why, Genius: A Mosaic of One Hundred Exemplary Creative Minds, Hamlet: Poem Unlimited, Where Shall Wisdom Be Found?,* and *Jesus and Yahweh: The Names Divine.* In 1999, Professor Bloom received the prestigious American Academy of Arts and Letters Gold Medal for Criticism. He has also received the International Prize of Catalonia, the Alfonso Reyes Prize of Mexico, and the Hans Christian Andersen Bicentennial Prize of Denmark.

James Ellis was emeritus professor of English at the University of North Carolina at Greensboro.

Ronald Weber is professor emeritus of American studies at the University of Notre Dame.

Peter Wolfe is the author of numerous works on literary figures, including *Craft and Vision in William Gaddis; The Art of John Le Carre; Yukio Mishima;* and *The Disciplined Heart: Iris Murdoch and Her Novels.*

Marvin E. Mengeling was emeritus professor of English at Wisconsin State University in Oshkosh.

Paul Witherington taught at the University of the Pacific in Stockton, California.

James L. McDonald was professor of English at the University of Detroit Mercy.

James M. Mellard is a professor at Northern Illinois University. He is the author of *Using Lacan, Reading Fiction* (1991).

Gordon E. Slethaug is a professor of English at the University of Hong Kong. He is the author of *The Play of the Double in Postmodern American Fiction* and *Beautiful Chaos: Chaos Theory and Metachaotics in Recent American Fiction*, and is coauthor of *Understanding John Barth*.

James Holt McGavran is professor of English at the University of North Carolina, Charlotte.

Milton P. Foster was a professor of English at Eastern Michigan University.

H.B. Bryant is professor of English at Clemson University where he teaches American and British literature of the Victorian period. He is the author of *A Separate Peace: The War Within* (1990).

David G. Holborn taught English at the University of Wisconsin, Stevens Point.

 Acknowledgments

James Ellis, excerpt from "*A Separate Peace:* The Fall from Innocence," *The English Journal*, vol. LIII, no. 5, May 1964, pp. 313–318. Reprinted with permission.

Ronald Weber, "Narrative Method in *A Separate Peace.*" From *studies in Short Fiction* 3, no. 1 (Fall 1965): pp. 63–72. © by Newberry College.

Peter Wolfe, "The Impact of Knowles's *A Separate Peace,*" coyright © 1970 by Peter Wolfe. First published in *The University Review* (*New Letters*) 36, no. 3 (Spring 1970): 189–198. It is printed here with the permission of *New Letters* and the Curators of the University of Missouri-Kansas City.

Marvin E. Mengeling, "*A Separate Peace:* Meaning and Myth." From *The English Journal* 58, no. 9 (December 1969): pp. 1322–1329. Reprinted by permission.

Paul Witherington, "*A Separate Peace:* A Study in Structural Ambiguity." From *The English Journal* 54, no. 9 (December 1965): pp. 795–800. Reprinted by permission.

James L. McDonald, "The Novels of John Knowles." Reprinted from *Arizona Quarterly* 25.4 (1967) pp. 335–342 by permission of the Regents of The University of Arizona.

James M. Mellard, "Counterpoint and 'Double Vision' in *A Separate Peace,*" from *Studies in Short Fiction* 4, no. 2 (Winter 1967): pp. 127–134. © 1967 by Newberry College.

Gordon E. Slethaug, "The Play of the Double in *A Separate Peace,*" from *The Canadian Review of American Studies,* vol. 15, no. 3 (Fall 1984): pp. 259–270. Used by permission of University of Toronto Press.

James Holt McGavran, "Fear's Echo and Unhinged Joy: Crossing Homosocial Boundaries in *A Separate Peace*," *Children's Literature*, 2002, vol. 30, pp. 67–80. Reprinted by permission of Yale University Press.

Milton P. Foster, "Levels of Meaning in *A Separate Peace*," from *The English Record*, vol. 18, no. 4 (April 1968): pp. 34–40. Reprinted by permission of New York State English Council.

H.B. Bryant, "Phineas's Pink Shirt in John Knowles' *A Separate Peace*," from *Notes on Contemporary Literature*, vol. 14, no. 5 (November 1984): pp. 5–6. Reprinted by permission.

David G. Holborn, "A Rationale for Reading John Knowles' *A Separate Peace*," from *Censored Books: Critical Viewpoints*, edited by N. Karolides, L. Burress, J. Kean, The Scarecrow Press, 1993, pp. 5–6. Reprinted by the Scarecrow Press, a division of Roman & Littlefield.

Index